W9-CHQ-482
Solaris 2.5
Command Summary

by Specialized Systems Consultants, Inc. (SSC)

1

ED COMMANDS

Many commands are of the form *address command*. **In** these commands, the items in parentheses indicate default address values.

Two values separated by a comma indicate an address range.

re refers to a regular expression (see Page 173)

nre refers to a new (replacement) regular expression.

Addresses:

.	current line
$	last line
n	*n*th line
'*x*	line marked as *x* with **k** command
/*re*/	first line (forward) *re*
?*re*?	first line (backward) *re*

Commands: (default addresses shown in ( ))

(**.**)**a**	append; end with period alone on a line
(**.,.**)**c**	change; end with period alone on a line
(**.,.**)**d**	delete lines
e [*file*]	edit *file*
E [*file*]	edit *file*; no diagnostics
f [*file*]	set current filename
(**1,$**)**g**/*re*/*cmds*	global on matching lines
(**1,$**)**G**/*re*/*cmds*	interactive global
h	explain last **?** diagnostic
H	toggle explanatory diagnostics mode
(**.**)**i**	insert; end with period alone on a line
(**.,.+1**)**j**	join lines
(**k**)*x*	set mark *x* at addressed line
(**.,.**)**l**	list displaying special characters
(**.,.**)**m***a*	move lines after line *a*
(**.,.**)**n**	print with line numbers
(**.,.**)**p**	print lines
P	toggle * prompt
q	quit
Q	quit, discarding any changes
(**$**)**r** [*file*]	read *file*
(**.,.**)**s**/*re*/*nre*/	substitute *nre* for *re*
(**.,.**)**s**/*re*/*nre*/**g**	like above but all occurrences in line
(**.,.**)**s**/*re*/*nre*/*n*	only match *n*th occurrence of *re*
(**.,.**)**t***a*	copy lines after line *a*
u	undo previous substitution
(**1,$**)**v**/*re*/*cmds*	like **g** but unmatched lines
(**1,$**)**V**/*re*/*cmds*	like **G** but unmatched lines
(**1,$**)**w** [*file*]	write [to file]
X	encrypt during **e**, **r** or **x**
(**$**) **=**	print line number
!*cmd*	execute *cmd* as UNIX command
(**.+1**)\<nl\>	print specified line

Note: If *file* (in **e**, **E** or **r**) begins with **!**, it is a UNIX command whose output is input to the edit buffer. In **w**, **!***file* uses buffer as input to command.

2

UNIX / Solaris 2.5 Command Summary

This booklet is designed as a reference for experienced UNIX users and as a learning tool for newcomers. It is based primarily on contents of the Solaris 2.5 SunOS Reference Manual, Section 1, on User Commands for Solaris 2.5 with some system administration, network administration, and superuser commands excluded. Some other standard commands are included from other Solaris 2.5 sections when they seem to be useful to the normal user.

Four special sections cover details of specific commands:

Usage Notes

Command names are organized alphabetically.

Each command description consists of a title line (with a short definition in English), one or more invocation lines (showing overall syntax and in some cases the directory location of the binary for the command), and syntax descriptions of the command's options and arguments.

- A % is used to represent the system prompt and is not typed by the user
- **Boldface** is used to represent items which must be typed exactly as shown
- *Italics* are used to represent items that are to be substituted for (such as filenames)
- Brackets [ ] surround items that are optional; do not type the brackets (unless otherwise specified)

The following special abbreviations are used to minimize redundant text:

- **stdin** represents the standard input: by default, this is the terminal keyboard
- **stdout** represents the standard output: by default this is the terminal screen
- **stderr** represents the standard error: by default, this is the terminal screen
- *option* represents the selection of an option from the list following the command line
- *file* represents a file name
- *arg* represents an argument
- Plurals (i.e. *options*, *files* or *args*) imply that multiple occurrences are permitted
- Numbered arguments (e.g. *file1*, *file2*) indicate a precise number of occurrences is required
- Options that take arguments generally need to be entered separately from other options with their arguments immediately following

Further Usage Notes

For the shell to parse a command line correctly, the arguments must be separated by whitespace or punctuation. Whitespace consists of one or more space characters, tab characters and/or the end of line character.

In many commands, use of spaces between option letters and the following words is optional. For example, both **– o** *file* and **–o***file* may be valid.

Many commands accept – – as an optional flag to indicate the end of the option list. This is useful where a file name begins with a dash.

In some cases, it may be necessary to quote arguments to commands in order to protect special characters from interpretation by the shell. See the shell section of this Command Summary or the SSC Pocket Tutorial on the shell for more information.

Special Flags

BSD compatability commands are flagged with a β

C shell versions of shell commands are flagged with a ξ

FACE/FMLI commands are flagged with a ϕ

KornShell commands are flagged with a κ

proc tools are flagged with a π

Solaris shell commands (similar to Bourne Shell) are flagged with a σ

Disclaimer and Bug Reports

Mail bug reports to SSC (see Page 1 for address) or send them electronically to **bugs@ssc.com**. For bug reports and constructive comments, you will have our enthusiastic appreciation.

For information on SSC products and services, we can be contacted electronically at **sales@ssc.com**.

SSC's URL is http://www.ssc.com.

ACCTCOM — Process Accounting

% **acctcom** [*options*] [*files*]

    if no *files* specified, reads from **/var/adm/pacct**;

    if **stdin** is a terminal or **/dev/null**, reads **stdin**

Options:

– a	also print average statistics
– b	read backwards, most recent commands first
– C *n*	only processes with CPU time $> n$ seconds
– e *time*	only processes existing at or before *time*
– E *time*	only processes ending at or before *time*
– f	print **fork/exec** flag and exit status
– g *group*	only processes of *group* (group *id* or *name*)
– h	print "hog factor," (CPU/elapsed time)
– H *factor*	only processes exceeding "hog factor"
– i	print I/O counts
– I *chars*	only processes transferring $>$ *chars*
– k	print kcore-minutes instead of memory size
– l *line*	only processes on **/dev/term/***line*
– m	print mean core size (default)
– n *pat*	only commands matching pattern *pat*
– o *output*	put records in *output*, not on **stdout**
– O *n*	only processes with sys CPU $> n$ seconds
– q	only print average statistics
– r	print "CPU factor," (user/(sys+user) time)
– s *time*	only processes existing at or after *time*
– S *time*	only processes starting at or after *time*
– t	separate user and system CPU times
– u *user*	only processes of *user* (user ID,login name, # (superuser), **?** (unknown user ID))
– v	don't print column headings
time	*hr* [:*min* [:*sec*]]

ADB — General Purpose Debugger

% **adb** [*option*] [*objfile* [*corefile*]]

Options:

– I *dirlst*	read files from colon separated list of directories with **$<** or **$<<** from *dir* (**/usr/platform/***plat-name***/lib/adb:/usr/lib/adb** default)
– k	perform kernel memory mapping
– P *prompt*	set **adb** prompt
– *mode*	set disassembly and register display mode
– w	open both *objfile* and *corefile* for update

Arguments:

objfile	executable file (**a.out** default)
corefile	core image dump file (**core** default)

(continued)

ADB, continued

Request format:

    [address] [,count] [command][;]
    address and count are expressions
    address   set . to address (**0** default)
    count   **1** default

Command Format: *verb* [*modifiers*]

Verbs (a subset):
    <newline>
                 repeat previous command with *count* = **1**
    ?*fmt*   print from *address* in *objfile* in specified *fmt*
    /*fmt*   print from *address* in *corefile* in specified
                 fmt
    =*fmt*   print value of *address* in specified *fmt*
    ?w *values* write 2 byte *value* to current
                 location in *objfile*
    /w *values* write 2 byte *value* to current
                 location in *corefile*
    ?W *values* write 4 byte *value* to current
                 location in *objfile*
    /W *values* write 4 byte *value* to current
                 location in *corefile*
    >*name*   assign value of dot to name
    !*cmd*   call new shell to execute *cmd*

Modifiers (a subset):
    $<*file*   switch command input to *file*
    $>*file*   append output to *file*
    $b   print all breakpoints
    $c   print C backtrace
    $d   set default radix to *address*
    $e   print external variable values and names
    $m   print address map
    $q   exit from **adb**
    $r   print registers and current instruction
    $v   print non-zero variables in octal
    $x   print names and contents of floating
                 point registers 0 - 15
    $X   print names and contents of floating
                 point registers 16 - 31
    :b*cmd*   set breakpoint, execute *cmd* when
                 encountered
    :c*signal* continue process sending it *signal*
    :d   delete breakpoint at *address*
    :k   kill current subprocess
    :r   run *objfile* as subprocess
    :s*signal* like **c** but single step *count* times

ADDBIB — Create/Extend Bibliographic Database
% **addbib** [*options*] *database*
Options:
     −a   suppress abstract prompt
     −p *promptfile*
                use *promptfile* as prompting skeleton
                where file consists of prompts, a TAB and
                key letters
     database   database to create or extend

ADMIN — Administer SCCS Files
% **admin** [*options*] *files*
     names of SCCS files read from **stdin** if *files* is −
     files either begin with **s.** or are directories
Options:
     −a*ident*   authorize *ident* (username or group ID
                number) to make **delta**s
     −b   force encoding of binary data
     −d*flag*   delete specified flag (see **−f**)
     −e*ident*   erase *ident*'s (username or group ID
                number) **delta** authorization
     −f*flag*[*val*]   set flags with optional values:
                b   permit branch deltas
                c*high*   set highest release (**9999** default)
                d*n*   set **get**'s default delta number
                f*low*   set lowest release (**1** default)
                i[*str*]   fatal error if no ID keywords or no
                          keywords matching optional *str*
                j   permit multiple **get**s at once
                l*list*   lock releases not to be edited
                          list is comma-delimited;
                          a means all
                m*text*   *text* replaces ID keyword **%M%**
                n   make null deltas for
                          skipped releases
                q*text*   *text* replaces ID keyword **%Q%**
                t*text*   *text* replaces ID keyword **%Y%**
                v[*file*]   **delta**s request Modification
                          Request numbers, *file* is a
                          checking program
     −h   verify file integrity via SCCS checksum
     −i[*file*]   source for new file (**stdin** default)
                (implies **−n**). Only one **−i** per
                admin command
     −m[*list*]   *list* of Modification Numbers inserted
                as reason for first delta
     −n   create new SCCS file, file empty if no **−i**
     −r*n*   set initial release delta number to *n*
     −t[*file*]   source of descriptive text
                (required with **−i** and **−n**),
                if no *file* descriptive text removed
     −y[*text*]   *text* is comment for initial
                delta valid only with **−i** or **−n**
     −z   "correct" checksum ignoring
                file corruption

ALIAS — Create or Display Pseudonym(s) for Command(s)
% **/usr/bin/alias** [*name* [=*str*]...]

name	alias name
str	string value that replaces the alias name on evocation

ξ **ALIAS** — Create or Display Pseudonym(s) for Command(s)
% **alias** [*name* [*def*]]

name	alias name
def	what alias translates to

κ **ALIAS** — Create or Display Pseudonym(s) for Command(s)
% **alias** [*options*] [*name* [=*value*]]
Options:

−t	set or list tracked aliases
−x	set or print exported aliases
name	alias name
value	value alias translates to

β **APROPOS** — Locate Commands by Keyword Lookup
% **apropos** *keywords*

AR — Maintain Archives and Libraries
% **/usr/bin/ar** [−**V**] − *key afile files*
% **/usr/xpg4/bin/ar** [−**V**] − *key afile files*

−**V**	print version information

key is one character from the set **dmpqrtx** and optionally one or more from **abcCisTuv**

−**a**	new files positioned after *key* file
−**b**	new files positioned before *key* file
−**c**	create *afile* without message
−**C**	Prevent overwrite of files in extraction of files
−**d**	delete *files* from *afile*
−**i**	same as - **b**
−**m**[*pc posname*]	move *files* to specified place (end of file default)
−**p**	print *files* in *afile*
−**q**	quickly append *files* to end of *afile*
−**r**[*option*][*pc posname*]	replace *files*
	u only update if newer
−**s**	create symbol table
−**t**	print table of contents of *afile* (all *files* default)
−**T**	Provide required file name truncation
−**u**	update older files
−**v**	verbose
−**x**	extract *files*

(continued)

AR, continued

pc	positioning character (used with **r** or **m**)
	a after *posname*
	b before *posname*
	i before *posname*
posname	name of file in archive, used to specify where to move files

afile   name of archive or library

ARCH — Display Host Architecture
% **/usr/bin/arch** [**-k**] [*archname*]

     – k   display the kernal architecture

AS — SPARC Assembler
% **as** [*options*] *file*
Options:

– b	enable Sun SourceBrowser
– D*name*[=*def*]	pass to **cpp** without interpreting (requires **– P**)
– I*path*	pass to **cpp** without interpreting (requires **– P**)
– KPIC	generate position-independent code
– L	save all symbols in ELF symbol table
– m	run input through **m4** preprocessor; with **– m** keywords cannot be used as symbols in input file
– n	suppress warnings
– o *output*	name of output file (*file*.**o** default)
– P	run **cpp** on files being assembled
– q	quick assembly; don't build node list; (disables many error checks)
– Qn	suppress tool ID information (default)
– Qy	put tool ID information in output
– s	don't strip **.stab** sections in static linker
– S	produce disassembly of code to **stdout**
– S[C]	same as **– S** but don't include comment lines in output
– T	interpret symbol names in 4.x assembly files as 5.x symbol names
– U*name*	pass name to **cpp** when -P is specified, otherwise ignore
– V	print version information
– xarch=*verspec*	
	verspec is one of the following version specifiers:
	v7 SPARK V7, ELF
	v8 SPARK V8, ELF
	v8a SPARK V8 no quad floats nor fsmuld, ELF
	v8plus SPARK V9, works >=V8+, no quad floats, ELF

(continued)

9

AS, continued

> v8plusa SPARC V9 with VIS, no quad
> floats, >=V8+, V8+ ELF

   –xF   use SPARC works analyzer to generate
> additional info for performance analysis
> of executable

cpp is a C preprocessor.

AS — x86 Assembler
% **as** [*options*] *file*
Options:

–m	run input through **m4** preprocessor
–n	suppress warnings
–o *output*	name of output file (*file*.**o** default)
–P	run **cpp** on files being assembled
–D*name*[*=def*]	
	pass to **cpp** without interpreting (requires **–P**)
–I*path*	pass to **cpp** without interpreting (requires **–P**)
–Qn	suppress tool ID information (default)
–Qy	put tool ID information in output
–s	don't strip **.stab** sections in static linker
–U*name*	pass name to **cpp** when -P is specified, otherwise ignore
–V	print version information

ASA — Display Host Architecture
% **asa** [**-f**] [**files**]

   –f   start each file on new page

AT — Execute Commands Later
% **at** [*options*] [*time*] [*day*] [+*n unit*] [*jobid*]
   add queue entry
Options:

–c	**csh** to execute at-job
–f *script*	read commands from *script*
–k	ksh to execute at-job
–m	send mail to user after completion
–q *queue*	submit job in *queue*
–s	**sh** (standard Bourne Shell) to execute at-job
–t *time time*	
	option argument specifies time (in touch command format) to start the at-job
day	month name followed by date, day of week, **today** or **tomorrow** (some abbreviations accepted)
n unit	*n* **minutes**, **hours**, **days**, **weeks**, **months** or **years**
time	1-4 digits and optional **am**, **pm**, **zulu** (GMT) or **noon**, **midnight**, **now** or **next**

(continued)

AT, continued
% **at** [option]   check queue status
Options:
    −l [jobs]   display job numbers of submitted jobs
    −r jobs   remove jobs scheduled by **at** or **batch**

ATQ — Display "at" Queue in Execution Order
% **atq** [option] [usernames]
Options:
    −c   display in order submitted
    −n   display only number of jobs in queue

ATRM — Remove Jobs From "at" Queue
% **atrm** [option] [args]
Options:
    −a   all jobs for current user
    −f   suppress removal information (force)
    −i   prompt to verify before
        removal (interactive)

args can be user names and/or job numbers

AUDIOCONVERT — Convert Audio File Formats
% **audioconvert** [options] [files]
stdin read if − or no files specified
Options:
    −?   print options list
    −f outfmt output file format
    −F   force input files to be treated as specified
        by a **−i** option
    −o outfile concatenated, converted output
        written to outfile
        (output to **stdout** if no **−o** or **−p** option)
    −p   in-place conversion; overwrites input

files input file names optionally preceeded by
    input format specifications of the form:
                −i formspec
    where formspec is a comma-delimited list of:
                keyword=value
    keyword is any of:
                rate   audio sampling rate (sample
                        per second)
                channels
                      number of interleaved channels
                encoding
                      encoding format (**ulaw**, **alaw**,
                      linear8,linear16,linear32, **pcm**,
                      g721, **g723**, **voice**, **cd**, **dat**)
                format data format (**sun**, **raw**)
                offset byte offset to data (**-i** only)

AUDIOPLAY — Play Audio Files
% **audioplay** [options] [files]
stdin read if − or no files specified
Options:
    −?   print options list

(continued)

AUDIOPLAY, continued

−b *bal*	set audio balance	
	(**−100** = left, **0** = center, **100** = right)	
−d *dev*	device to receive output	
	(**AUDIODEV** env variable if not specified,	
	or **/dev/audio**)	
−i	return immediately if device is busy	
−p *port*	specify output port (**speaker**,	
	headphone, **line**)	
−v *vol*	output volume level (**0** to **100**)	
−V	verbose	

Search path for audiofiles is set by colon-separated list assigned to env variable **AUDIOPATH**

AUDIORECORD — Record Audio File
% **audiorecord** [*options*] [*file*]
Options:

−?	print options list
−a	append data to *file*
−b *bal*	set audio balance
−c *chan*	channels (**1**, **2**, **mono**, **stereo**)
	(**−100** = left, **0** = center, **100** = right)
−d *dev*	device to receive output
	(**AUDIODEV** env variable if not specified,
	or **/dev/audio**)
−e *enc*	data encoding format (**alaw**, **ulaw**,
	linear; **ulaw** default)
−f	sample rate must match current data
	in file (with **−a**)
−i *info*	put *info* in header
−m *vol*	monitor volume level (**0** to **100**)
−p *port*	specify input port (**mic**, **line**, **internal-cd**)
−s *rate*	samples per second (**8k** default)
−t *time*	maximum recording time in seconds or
	hh:*mm*:*ss*.*dd*
−v *vol*	recording gain (**0** to **100**)

AWK — Pattern Scanning Language (See Pages 163-167)
% **/usr/bin/awk** [*options*] [*'prog'*] [*params*] [*files*]
% **/usr/xpg4/bin/awk** [*options*] [*'prog'* | **-f** *pfile*] [*args*]
    stdin read if **−** or no *files* specified
Options:

−f *pfile*	use *pfile* as program
−F*c*	field separator character is *c*

prog	program line (should be in single quotes)
params	form **x**=..., **y**=...

BANNER — Print Banner with Large Letters
% **banner** *strings*

string	10 characters maximum each

BASENAME — Delete Prefix and Suffix from Pathname
% **/usr/bin/basename** *string* [*suffix*]
β % **/usr/ucb/basename** *string* [*suffix*]
% **/usr/xpg4/bin/basename** *string* [*suffix*]

string   pathname to filter
suffix   optional suffix to delete

BATCH — Run Command When System Load Permits
% **batch**
    stdin queued as background job

BC — Unlimited Precision Arithmetic Language
% **bc** [*option*] [*files*]
    stdin read after all *files*
Options:
    – c   compile only
    – l   math library (sin, exp, log, arctan, Bessel)

BDIFF — Compare Big Files
% **bdiff** *file1 file2* [*options*]
    stdin read if **–** specified for *file1* or *file2*
Options:
    n   set size of split segments to *n*
               (**3500** default)
    – s   suppress diagnostics

ξκσ **BG** — Resume Execution in Background
See **Job Control** in Solaris SHELL section Pages 168-172

β **BIFF** — Incoming Mail Notification Control
% **/usr/ucb/biff** [*option*]
Options:
    n   turn off mail notification
    y   turn on mail notification
with no option, current status is displayed

ξ **BREAK** — Escape from Controlling Loop
% **break**

κσ **BREAK** — Escape from Controlling Loop
% **break** [*n*]

CAL — Print Calendar
% **cal** [[*month*] *year*]

month   number between 1 and 12
            (current month default)
year   number between 1 and 9999 (full year default)

CALENDAR — Reminder Service
% **calendar** [*option*]
Option:
    –   check everyone's **calendar** file and mail
                   items for today and tomorrow

DATEMASK environment variable can be set to
full pathname of format template where:

%B	full month name
%e	day of month
%y	year (4 digits)

CANCEL — Cancel Printer Requests Made By **lp**
% **cancel** [*ids*] [*printer*]
% **cancel –u** *login* [*printer*]

κσ **CASE** — Structured Conditional
See **Control Commands** in the Solaris SHELL section
Pages 168-172

CAT — Concatenate and Print Files
% **cat** [*options*] [*files*]
    stdin read if **–** or no *files* specified
Options:

– b	like **– n** but don't number blank lines
– e	with **– v** shows **$** before each newline
– n	precede each line with line number
– s	silent about nonexistent files
– t	with **– v** shows tabs as **ˆI** and formfeeds as **ˆL**
– u	unbuffered output
– v	show non-printing characters (except tabs, newlines and formfeeds)

β **CC** — BSD Compatibility Package C Compiler
% **/usr/ucb/cc** [*options*] *files*
This command uses BSD compiler resources first.

The following options are for the **/usr/ucb/cc** command
only, and are in addition to those available with the
/usr/ucb/ucbcc link to the C compiler:

– I*dir*	add *dir* to front of include file search list
– L*dir*	add *dir* to front of library search list

CC — SPARCompiler C 4.0
% **cc** [*options*] *files*

Options:

– #	Verbose
– ###	Don't execute, show components
– A*name* [(*def*)]	associate *name* with *def* as if by **#assert**
– A –	forget predefined macros and assertions
– Bdynamic	link with **lib***x***.so** first

(continued)

CC, continued

– Bstatic	link with **lib**x**.a**
– c	suppress link edit; produce **.o** files
– C	preprocessor does not delete comments
– dn	static linking
– dy	dynamic linking (default)
– Dname[=def]	
	define name as def (**1** default)
– erroff=t	suppress warnings, specifying
	comma separated list with any of (tag,
	no%tag, %all, %none)
– errtags[**=yes/no**]	
	if yes, or no argument, specifies tags for
	error messages
– fast	use common set of performance options
– fd	report old style functions
– flags	print compile option summary
– fnofma	(PowerPC) Don't generate fmadd
	or fmsub instructions
– fnonstd	force nonstandard floating point
	arithmatic hardware initialization
– fns	(SPARC) use SPARC nonstandard floating
	point mode
– fround=r	(SPARC) use IEEE 754 rounding
	mode r (**nearest**, **negative**, **positive**,
	tozero)
– fsimple[=n]	
	(SPARC) allow optimizer to use
	simplifying floating point assumptions
– fsingle	use single-precision arithmetic
	(only -Xs and -Xt)
– fstore	(x86) use target precision of expressions
	on assignment
– ftrap=t	(SPARC) use IEEE 754 trap mode t
	t is a command separated list with any of
	%all, **common**, [**%no**]**division**,
	[**%no**]**inexact**,
	[**%no**]**invalid**, **%none**, [**%no**]**overflow**,
	[**%no**]**underflow**
– E	only preprocessor output to **stdout**
– g	generate **sdb** debugger info
– G	produce shared object instead of
	dynamic link
– h name	name a dynamic library for linker
– H	print pathname of each included file on
	stderr
– i	tell linker ignore LD_LIBRARY_PATH
– Idir	dir added to include search path
– J	(HP-UX) allow very large source files
– keeptmp	keep temporary files from compilation
– KPIC	generate position independent code
– Kpic	like -**KPIC** but with smaller global
	offset table
–l x	search **lib**x**.so** or **lib**x**.a**
–Ldir	dir added to library search list
– mc	remove duplicate strings from
	output files' .comment sections

(continued)

15

CC, continued

– misalign	(SPARC) allow proper loads and stores with misaligned data
– misalign2	
	(SPARC) allow proper loads and stores with half-word aligned data
– mr	remove all strings from output files' .comment sections
– mr,*str*	remove all strings and append *str* to output files' .comment sections
– mt	specify multithread necessary options
– native	(SPARC) use available code generation options
– native	(x86) (PowerPC) generate code for available processor
– nofstore	(x86) turn **-fstore** off
– noqueue	disable compiler license request queuing
– o *output*	name of output file (**a.out** default)
– O	optimize object code produced
– p	set-up object files for profiling
– P	only preprocessor output to *files*.**i**
– qp	collect data for profiling
– Qn	suppress tool ID information
– Qy	put tool ID information in output (default)
– R*dir*[:*dir*]	specify library search directories to runtime linker
– s	tell linker to strip symbolic information
– S	put assembler source in *files*.**s** only
– U*symb*	remove initial definition of *symb*
– v	perform strict semantic checks
– V	print version information
– W *pass*, *arg1*[,*args*]	
	give arguments to *pass*

pass	one or more of **p012al**	
	0	compiler
	2	optimizer
	a	assembler
	c	C code generator
	l	link editor
	m	mcs
	p	preprocessor

–w	suppress warnings
–x386	(x86) optimize for 386 processor
–x486	(x86) optimize for 486 processor
–x601	(PowerPC) optimize for 601 processor
–x603	(PowerPC) optimize for 603 processor
–x604	(PowerPC) optimize for 604 processor
–xa	collect data for basic block profiling
–xarch=*a*	limit set of instructions compiler may use to *a*, including: **generic**, **v7**, **v8**, **v8a**, **v8plus**, **v8plusa**
–xautopar	(SPARC) generate parallelized code (automatic only)
–xCC	accept C++ comments

(continued)

CC, continued

–xcache=_c_ define cache properties _c_
which must be one of: _generic_ or
_s1/l1/a1_ or _s1/l1/a1:s2/l2/a2_ or
_s1/l1/a1:s2/l2/a2:s3/l3/a3_
where:

_si_	size of data cache at level _i_ in kilobytes
_li_	line size of data cache at level _i_ in bytes
_ai_	associativity of data cache at level _i_

–xcg89 (SPARC) macro for:
  -xarch=v7 -xchip=old -xcache=64/32/1
–xcg92 (SPARC) macro for:
  -xarch=v8 -xchip=super
  -xcache=16/64/4:1024/4/1
–xchip=_c_ specify _c_ as target processor
this may be: _generic_, _old_, _super_,
super2, _micro_, _micro2_, _hyper_,
hyper2, _powerup_, _ultra_
–xdepend (SPARC) enable all dependence-based
transformations
–xe do only syntax and symantic checking
–xexplicitpar
(SPARC) generate parallelized code
(explicit only)
–xF generate code for use with analyzer
–xhelp=_f_ display online help, where _f_
may be **flags**, **readme**, **errors**
–xildoff turn incremental linker off
–xildon turn incremental linker on
–xinline=[_f1,...,fn_]
attempt to inline _f1,...,fn_
–xlibmieee
use IEEE 754 return values for math
routines on exceptions
–xlibmil execute faster by inlining some
library routines
–xlicinfo return licensing system status
–xloopinfo(SPARC) show parallelized loops
–xM generate makefile dependencies
–xM1 generate makefile dependencies, but
exclude **/usr/include** tree
–xMerge merge data segment into text segment
–xnolib do not provide default libraries to linker
–xnolibmil
reset **-fast** to not include inline templates
–xO_n_ (SPARC) generate optimized code,
where _n_ is:

1	basic peephole optimization
2	basic local and global optimization
3	same as 2 with definitions for externals
4	same as 3 with automatic inline functions
5	highest level op optimization

(continued)

CC, continued

−xOn	(x86) (PowerPC) (HP-UX) generate optimized code, where n is defined as above.
−xP	print K&R C function definition prototypes
−xparallel	do parallel compilation
−xpentium	(x86) optimize for pentium processors
−xpg	prep object code for profiling
−xprofile\f(Sip)	collect data for profile or use a profile to optimize p (**collect**, **use:**name, **tcov**)
−xreduction	(SPARC) do reduction when generating parallelized code
−xregs=r	specify usage of registers in executables r may be a list of [**no%**]**appl**, [**no%**]**float**
−xrestrict=f	specify pointer valued function parameters as restricted where f may be function, **%all**, **%none**
−xs	put symbol tables for dbx in executable file
−xsave=mem	(SPARC) let compiler assume no memory based traps
−xsb	generate sourcebrowser info
−xsbfast	generate sourcebrowser info, don't compile
−xsfpconst	use single precision on unsuffixed float constants
−xspace	don't optimize in ways that increase code size
−xstrconst	put string literals in readonly data section of text segment
−xtarget=t	specify target system for instruction set and optimization; t may be **generic**, **native**, system
−xtempdir	set directory for temporary files
−xtime	report the execution time for each component
−xtransition	give warnings for loops that can't be parallelized
−xunroll	suggest optimizer unroll loops n times
−xvpara	(SPARC) warn of loops that can't be parallelized
−Xa	ANSI conformance but warn about promotion rule changes
−Xc	conformance − full ANSI (_ _**STDC**_ _ set to 1)
−Xs	warn if not K&R C code
−Xt	transition − accept compatible pre-ANSI code

(continued)

CC, continued

–Yc,dir	specify *dir* as directory for component *c* (see -**W** for possible values)
–YA,dir	set *dir* as default directory searched for components
–YI,dir	set *dir* as default directory searched for include files
–YP,dir	set *dir* as default directory for finding library files
–YS,dir	set *dir* as default directory startup object files
–Zll	create lock_lint database files
–Zlp	(SPARC) generate profile info on all loops
–Ztha	Prep code for analysis by Thread Analyzer

CD — Change Directory Utility
% **/usr/bin/cd** [*dir*]
    Environment variable **HOME** used if no *dir*
dir directory specified to become new working directory
PWD holds value of present working directory

ξ **CD** — Change Directory
% **cd** [*dir*]
    HOME used if no *dir*
If *dir* is a relative directory, the value of **CDPATH**
environment variable is used as a delimited list of
directories to search for *directory*.
PWD is set after each call to cd.

κ **CD** — Change Directory
% **cd** [*dir*]
    (behavior similar to σ)
% **cd** *old new*
    substitute string *new* for string *old* in
    directory spec.

σ **CD** — Change Directory
% **cd** [*dir*]
    HOME used if no *dir*
If *dir* is a relative directory, the value of **CDPATH**
environment variable is used as a delimited list of
directories to search for *directory*.
PWD is set after each call to cd.

CDC — Change SCCS Delta Comments
% **cdc** [*options*] *files*
    SCCS filenames read from **stdin** if *files* is –
Options:

– mlist	add modification request numbers, remove any preceded with an exclamation mark (!)
– rsid	specify SCCS ID of delta to change
– y[text]	replace comment with *text*

CFLOW — Build C Flowgraph
% **cflow** [*options*] *files*
Options:
–d *n*	cut off flow graph at depth *n*
–i_	include names starting with _
–ix	include static data and external symbols (functions only default)
–r	produce inverted listing

Note: C preprocessor **cpp** options are accepted by **cflow**. This is the 2.1 documentation of **cflow** as it is not included in the 2.5 documentation and may not be available with default command set.

CHECKEQ — Check **eqn** Input
% **checkeq** [*files*]
    stdin read if no *files* specified

CHECKNR — N /Troff Error Checker
% **checknr** [*options*] [*files*]
    stdin read if no *files* specified
Options:
–a*macropairs*	check each *macropair* (e.g. **.DS.DE**) for balance (must be two letter names)
–c *macroids*	don't complain if *macroids* (e.g. .XA.XM.AX) are undefined (must be two letter names)
–f	ignore \f font changes
–s	ignore \s size changes

κ **CHDIR** — Same as CD for sh and csh

CHGRP — Change Group ID of Files (See **CHOWN**)
% **chgrp** [*options*] *group files*
Options:
–f	force change, no error messages
–h	change group of symbolic link (not file)
–R	recursive through subdirectories

group   group name or decimal group ID

CHKEY — Change User Encryption Key
% **chkey** [*option*] [*files*]
Options:
–p	re-encrypt existing key with users login password
–s nis	update NIS database
–s nisplus	update NIS+ database

group   group name or decimal group ID

CHMOD — Change Access Modes

% **chmod** [*option*] *mode files*

Option:

– f	force change, no error messages
– R	recursively descend through directories

mode can be numeric or symbolic. The symbolic case consists of the form [**agou**][**+ – =**][**glorstuwx**] where:

a	group, other and user access permissions (default)
g	group access permissions
o	other access permissions
u	user access permissions
+	add the permission to status of *files*
–	remove the permission from status of *files*
=	set the permission of *files* to specified value
l	mandatory locking
r	read permission
s	set owner ID or group ID on execution
t	save text mode; file owner only delete for directories
w	write permission
x	execute permission

g, **o** or **u** after the **=** uses the **g**roup, **o**ther or **u**ser permission as a model

Multiple symbolic modes are separated by commas

The numeric case is formed from:

4000	set user ID on execution
20X0	set group ID on execution if X is **7**, **5**, **3**, **1** set mandatory locking if x is **6**, **4**, **2**, **0** (use symbolic mode to set or clear if *file* is directory)
1000	save text image after execution (sticky bit)
0X00	owner's permission, where X is OR of: 04 (read), 02 (write), 01 (execute)
00X0	group's permission
000X	other's permission

CHOWN — Change Owner of Files

% **chown** [*options*] *owner*[*.group*] *files*

Options:

– f	do not report errors
– h	change owner of symbolic link (not file)
– R	recursive through subdirectories

owner   owner name or decimal user ID

β CHOWN — Change Owner of Files

% **chown** [*options*] *owner*[*.group*] *files*

Options:

– f	suppress error messages
– R	recursive through subdirectories

(continued)

CHOWN, continued

owner	owner name or decimal user ID
group	group name or decimal group ID

CKDATE — Prompt For and Validate Date
% **ckdate** [*options*]
Options:

- **d** *default*
  use *default* if no user input
- **e** *errmsg*
  set error message to *errmsg*
- **f** *fmt*   input format:

%b	abbreviated month name
%B	full month name
%d	day of month (01-31)
%D	date as %m/%d/%y (default)
%e	day of month (1-31)
%h	same as **%b%**
%m	month number (01-12)
%y	year within century
%Y	year (4 digits)

- **h** *hlpmsg*
  set help message to *hlpmsg*
- **k** *pid*   send signal to *pid* if
  user aborts command
- **p** *prompt*
  use *prompt* as prompt
- **Q**   disallow quit as valid response
- **s** *signal*   send specified signal to *pid* in **−k**
  (**SIGTERM** default)
- **W** *width*   format messages to *width* characters

~ at the beginning or end of a message is replaced with the default message

Exit Status:

0	successful
1	EOF on input, negative width with -W, or usage error
3	user termination
4	garbled format argument

CKGID — Prompt For and Validate Group ID
% **ckgid** [*options*]
Options:

- **d** *default* use *default* if no user input
- **e** *errmsg* set error message to *errmsg*
- **h** *hlpmsg* set help message to *hlpmsg*
- **k** *pid*   send signal to *pid* if
  user aborts command
- **m**   display list of groups as help or
  error response
- **p** *prompt* use *prompt* as prompt
- **Q**   disallow quit as valid response
- **s** *signal*   send specified signal to *pid* in **−k**
  (**SIGTERM** default)
- **W** *width* format messages to *width* characters

(continued)

CKGID, continued

~ at the beginning or end of a message is replaced with the default message

Exit Status:

0	successful
1	EOF on input, negative width on -W, or usage error
3	user termination

CKINT — Prompt For and Validate Integer

% **ckint** [*options*]

Options:

– b	*base*	numeric base (2-36, **10** default)
– d	*default*	use *default* if no user input
– e	*errmsg*	set error message to *errmsg*
– h	*hlpmsg*	set help message to *hlpmsg*
– k	*pid*	send signal to *pid* if user aborts command
– p	*prompt*	use *prompt* as prompt
– Q		disallow quit as valid response
– s	*signal*	send signal to *pid* specified by **– k** option (**SIGTERM** default)
– W	*width*	format messages to *width* characters

~ at the beginning or end of a message is replaced with the default message

Exit Status:

0	successful
1	EOF on input, negative width on -W or usage error
3	user termination

CKITEM — Build Menu and Return Item

% **ckitem** [*options*] [*choices*]

Options:

– d	*default*	use *default* if no user input
– e	*errmsg*	set error message to *errmsg*
– f	*file*	display menu items in *file*
– h	*hlpmsg*	set help message to *hlpmsg*
– i	*invis*	specify invisible choice (valid but not displayed) (*invis* is comma-separated list)
– k	*pid*	send signal to *pid* if user aborts command
– l	*label*	print *label* above menu
– m	*max*	maximum number of choices
– n		don't display in alphabetical order
– o		return only one menu token
– p	*prompt*	use *prompt* as prompt
– Q		disallow quit as valid response
– s	*signal*	send specified signal to *pid* in **– k** (**SIGTERM** default)
– u		display items as unnumbered list
– W	*width*	format messages to *width* characters

choice a menu line item

(continued)

CKITEM, continued
~ at the beginning or end of a message is replaced with the default message

Exit Status:

0	successful
1	EOF on input, negative width on -W or usage error
3	user termination
4	no choices

CKKEYWD — Prompt For and Validate Keyword
% **ckkeywd** [*options*] [*keywords*]
Options:

– d	*default*	use *default* if no user input
– e	*errmsg*	set error message to *errmsg*
– h	*hlpmsg*	set help message to *hlpmsg*
– k	*pid*	send signal to *pid* if user aborts command
– p	*prompt*	use *prompt* as prompt
– Q		disallow quit as valid response
– s	*signal*	send specified signal to *pid* in **– k** (**SIGTERM** default)
– W	*width*	format messages to *width* characters

keywords   list against which to verify answer

~ at the beginning or end of a message is replaced with the default message

Exit Status:

0	successful
1	EOF on input or usage error
3	user termination

CKPATH — Prompt For and Validate Pathname
% **ckpath** [*options*]
Options:

– a		pathname must be absolute
– b		pathname must be block special file
– c		pathname must be character special file
– d	*default*	use *default* if no user input
– e	*errmsg*	set error message to *errmsg*
– f		pathname must be regular file
– h	*hlpmsg*	set help message to *hlpmsg*
– k	*pid*	send signal to *pid* if user aborts command
– l		pathname must be relative
– n		pathname must not exist
– o		pathname must exist
– p	*prompt*	use *prompt* as prompt
– Q		disallow quit as valid response
– r		pathname must be readable
– s	*signal*	send specified signal to *pid* in **– k** (**SIGTERM** default)
– t		pathname must be touchable
– w		pathname must be writable
– W	*width*	format messages to *width* characters
– x		pathname must be executable

(continued)

CKPATH, continued
- **−y** pathname must be directory
- **−z** pathname must be non-zero size file

~ at the beginning or end of a message is replaced with the default message

Exit Status:

0	successful
1	EOF on input or usage error
2	mutually exclusive options
3	user termination
4	mutually exclusive options

CKRANGE — Prompt For and Validate Integer Range
% **ckrange** [*options*]

Options:
- **−b** *base* numeric base (**2-36**, **10** default)
- **−d** *default* use *default* if no user input
- **−e** *errmsg* set error message to *errmsg*
- **−h** *hlpmsg* set help message to *hlpmsg*
- **−k** *pid* send signal to *pid* if user aborts command
- **−l** *low* lower limit of range
- **−p** *prompt* use *prompt* as prompt
- **−Q** disallow quit as valid response
- **−s** *signal* send specified signal to *pid* in **−k** (**SIGTERM** default)
- **−u** *high* upper limit of range
- **−W** *width* format messages to *width* characters

~ at the beginning or end of a message is replaced with the default message

Exit Status:

0	successful
1	EOF on input, bad width or usage error
2	usage error
3	user termination

CKSTR — Prompt For and Validate String
% **ckstr** [*options*]

Options:
- **−d** *default* use *default* if no user input
- **−e** *errmsg* set error message to *errmsg*
- **−h** *hlpmsg* set help message to *hlpmsg*
- **−k** *pid* send signal to *pid* if user aborts command
- **−l** *len* maximum length of input
- **−p** *prompt* use *prompt* as prompt
- **−Q** disallow quit as valid response
- **−r** *regexp* match regular expression with input (multiple permitted; input only need match one)
- **−s** *signal* send specified signal to *pid* in **−k** (**SIGTERM** default)
- **−W** *width* format messages to *width* characters

(continued)

CKSTR, continued

˜ at the beginning or end of a message is replaced
with the default message

Exit Status:

0	successful
1	EOF on input, bad width or usage error
2	invalid regular expression
3	user termination

CKSUM — Write File Checksums and Sizes
% **cksum** [*files*]

CKTIME — Prompt For and Validate Time
% **cktime** [*options*]
Options:

–d	*default*	use *default* if no user input
–e	*errmsg*	set error message to *errmsg*
–f	*fmt*	input format:
	%H	hour (00-23)
	%I	hour (00-12)
	%M	minute (00-59)
	%p	AM or PM
	%r	time as **%I:%M:%S %p**
	%R	time as **%H:%M** (default)
	%S	seconds (00-59)
	%T	time as **%H:%M:%S**
–h	*hlpmsg*	set help message to *hlpmsg*
–k	*pid*	send signal to *pid* if user aborts command
–p	*prompt*	use *prompt* as prompt
–Q		disallow quit as valid response
–s	*signal*	send specified signal to *pid* in **–k** (**SIGTERM** default)
–W	*width*	format messages to *width* characters

˜ at the beginning or end of a message is replaced
with the default message

Exit Status:

0	successful
1	EOF on input, bad width or usage error
3	user termination
4	garbled format argument

CKUID — Prompt For and Validate User ID
% **ckuid** [*options*]
Options:

–d	*default*	use *default* if no user input
–e	*errmsg*	set error message to *errmsg*
–h	*hlpmsg*	set help message to *hlpmsg*
–k	*pid*	send signal to *pid* if user aborts command
–m		display list of valid logins as help

(continued)

CKUID, continued
- **−p** *prompt* use *prompt* as prompt
- **−Q**   disallow quit as valid response
- **−s** *signal*   send specified signal to *pid* in **−k** (**SIGTERM** default)
- **−W** *width* format messages to *width* characters

˜ at the beginning or end of a message is replaced with the default message

Exit Status:
0	successful
1	EOF on input, bad width or usage error
2	usage error
3	user termination

CKYORN — Prompt For and Validate Yes/No
% **ckyorn** [*options*]
Options:
- **−d** *default* use *default* if no user input
- **−e** *errmsg* set error message to *errmsg*
- **−h** *hlpmsg* set help message to *hlpmsg*
- **−k** *pid*   send signal to *pid* if user aborts command
- **−p** *prompt* use *prompt* as prompt
- **−Q**   disallow quit as valid response
- **−s** *signal*   send specified signal to *pid* in **−k** (**SIGTERM** default)
- **−W** *width* format messages to *width* characters

˜ at the beginning or end of a message is replaced with the default message

Exit Status:
0	successful
1	EOF on input, bad width or usage error
2	usage error
3	user termination

CLEAR — Clear Terminal Screen
% **clear**

CMP — Compare Two Files
% **cmp** [*options*] *file1 file2*
    stdin read if **−** specified for *file1*
Options:
−l	print byte number and bytes
−s	silent, return exit codes only

Exit Status:
0	files identical
1	files different
> 1	error

φ **COCHECK** — Check Co-process for Input
% **cocheck** *proc_id*

proc_id   the *command* or *id* from **cocreate**

ϕ **COCREATE** — Start Co-process

% **cocreate** [*options*] *command*

Options:

– e	*expect*	start of line from co-process that indicates EOF (newline default)
– i	*id*	alternate name of co-process being initialized (*id* defaults to *command* if no **– i** option)
– r	*path*	pathname FMLI will read from
– R	*refname*	local name for co-process
– s	*send*	string to append to all output sent to co-process
– w	*path*	pathname FMLI will write to

command   name of program to start as a co-process

ϕ **CODESTROY** — Terminate Co-process Pipes

% **codestroy** [*option*] *proc_id* [*string*]

Option:

– R	*refname*	local name for co-process

proc_id   the *command* or *id* from **cocreate**
string   string to send to co-process

COL — Filter Reverse Line-Feeds from **stdin**

% **col** [*options*]

Options:

– b	printer cannot backspace
– f	forward half linefeed okay
– p	don't ignore unknown ESC sequences
– x	don't convert whitespace to tabs

COMB — Combine SCCS Deltas

% **comb** [*options*] *files*

     SCCS filenames read from **stdin** if *files* is –

Options:

– c*list*	*list* of deltas to be preserved
– o	access as created file instead of most recent
– p*sid*	specify oldest delta to be preserved
– s	generate shell script to produce usage report

COMM — Select or Reject Common Lines

% **comm** [– *options*] *file1 file2*

     stdin read if – specified for *file1* or *file2*

Options:

1	suppress lines only from *file1*
2	suppress lines only from *file2*
3	suppress lines in both *file1* and *file2*

COMMAND — Execute or Interpret a Command
% **command** [*option*] *command* [*args*]
Options:

– p	use defaullt **PATH**
– v	echo path that would be used for command
– V	echo explanation of shell usage of command

COMPRESS — Compress Files
% **compress** [*options*] *files*
    stdin read if – specified for *file1* or *file2*
Options:

– b *bits*	upper limit of common substring codes (9 to 16; 16 default)
– c	write to **stdout** instead of *file*.**Z**
– f	force compression (no prompts)
– v	display compression percentage

ξ **CONTINUE** — Advance in a Loop
% **continue**

$\kappa\sigma$ **CONTINUE** — Advance in a Loop
% **continue** [*n*]

ϕ **CORECEIVE** — Read Input from Co-process
% **coreceive** *proc_id*

proc_id   the *command* or *id* from **cocreate**

ϕ **COSEND** — Send String to Co-process
% **cosend** [*option*] *proc_id string*
Option:

– n	don't wait for response

proc_id   the *command* or *id* from **cocreate**
string   string to send to co-process

CP — Copy Files
% **cp** [*options*] *file1 file2*
    make a copy of *file1* named *file2*
% **cp** *files directory*
    make copies of specified *files* in *directory*
Options:

– –	signifies end of options (optional)
– f	unlink destination file if filespec unreachable
– i	prompt before overwriting target
– p	preserve permissions and modification time
– r	recursively copy files and subdirectories
– R	like -r, but pipes replicated, not read from

CPIO — Copy Archives
% **cpio** – **i**[**6bBcCdEfHIkmMrRsStuvV**] [*patterns*]
    copy in: read **stdin**, select using *patterns*
% **cpio** – **o**[**aABcLvV**] –[**CHMO**]
    copy out: pathnames from **stdin** to **stdout**
% **cpio** – **p**[**adlLmuvV**] –[**R**] *dir*
    copy out and in: read **stdin**, copy to directory *dir*
Note that option -P is available but was not specified
in the syntax diagrams in the Solaris 2.5 manual.
Options:

– **6**		UNIX 6th edition format
– **a**		reset access times of input files after copy
– **A**		append to archive specified with – **O**
– **b**		swap bytes within each word
– **B**		5,120 bytes/record (for **/dev/rmt/***??* only)
– **c**		write header info as ASCII characters
– **C**	*size*	block to *size* bytes/record
– **d**		create directories as needed
– **E**	*file*	*file* contains list of filenames to extract
– **f**		copy all files not in *patterns*
– **H**	*hdr*	read or write header in specified format
		bar or **BAR** bar header and format
		crc or **CRC** ASCII w/expanded device numbers
		ustar or **USTAR** IEEE/P1003 standard
		tar or **TAR** tar format
		odc ASCII w/small device numbers
– **I**	*file*	read *file* as input archive
– **k**		skip corrupted headers
– **l**		link rather than copy whenever possible
– **L**		follow symbolic links
– **m**		retain previous file modification time
– **M**	*message*	
		message for media switch (**%d** can be used for sequence number)
– **O**	*file*	direct output to *file*
– **P**		preserve ACLs
– **r**		rename files interactively
– **s**		swap bytes
– **S**		swap halfwords
– **t**		print table of contents only
– **u**		copy disregarding age of files
– **v**		verbose, list filenames
– **V**		print dot for each file read/written

patterns	names of files to select, specified in shell notation (***** default)
dir	destination pathnames relative to this *dir*

CPP — run C preprocessor
% **cpp** [*options*] [*ifile* [*ofile2*]]
    make a copy of *file1* named *file2*
Options:

– **B**	support C++ comments

(continued)

CPP, continued

– C	pass through comments
– H	print include file names to stderr
– M	generate makefile depencency list to stdout
– p	use only first 8 characters to distinguish symbols; issue warning if extra tokens with directives
– P	don't produce line control information
– R	allow recursive macros
– T	use only first 8 characters in names (for compatibility only)
– undef	remove initial definitions
– D*sym=val*	
	define *sym* to be *val*
– D*sym*	same as **– D***sym=1*
– I*dir*	put *dir* in search path for **#include** files having relative filespecs
– U*sym*	remove initial definition of *sym*
– Y*dir*	use *dir* to search for **#include** files

CRONTAB — Manipulate Crontab File
% **crontab** [*file*]
    stdin read if no *file* specified
% **crontab** [*option* [**-u** *user*]]
Options:

– e	edit or create empty file
– l	list user's crontab file
– r	remove user's crontab file from **/usr/spool/cron**

CRYPT — Encrypt/Decrypt **stdin** to **stdout**
% **crypt** [*password*]
Argument:
    password is the key; if not given, it is prompted for
% **crypt** [**–k**]
    use value of env variable **CRYPTKEY** as key

CSCOPE — Interactively Examine C Program
% **cscope** [*options*] *files*
Options:

– b	build cross-reference only
– c	do not compress data
– C	ignore case when searching
– d	don't update cross reference
– e	suppress ˆe prompt between files
– f *file*	use *file* instead of **cscope.out**
– F *file*	read symbol reference lines from *file*
– i *file*	use *file* as list of source filenames
– I *dir*	search *dir* for include files
– l	enter line-oriented mode
– L	single search; used with – *n*
– n *pat*	go to input field *n* (0 is first) and search for *pat*
– p *n*	display last *n* components of path (**1 default**)

(continued)

CSCOPE, continued

– P *path*	prepend *path* to relative pathnames
– q	build inverted index for quick symbol searching
– s *dir*	look in *dir* for sources
– T	use only 8 characters in symbol match
– u	unconditionally build cross-reference
– U	don't check file timestamps
– V	print version information

ξ **CSH** — Invoke Shell With C-like Syntax

% **csh** [*options*] [*args*]

Options:

– b	force break in option processing
– c	read commands from first *arg*
– e	exit if command fails or non-zero exit status
– f	do not execute **.login** or **.cshrc**; speeds start of shell
– i	force interactive mode
– n	parse commands without executing them
– s	commands read from **stdin**
– t	execute one command line, then exit
– v	print input lines as read
– V	like **– v**, except enable before reading **.cshrc**
– x	print commands as executed, with arguments
– X	like **– x**, except enable before reading **.cshrc**

CSPLIT — Split File

% **csplit** [*options*] *file args*

Options:

– f *prefix*	name new files *prefix*00 ... *prefix*n (**xx**00 ... **xx**n default)
– k	leave created files if error
– s	suppress character counts

args	where to split *file*, of the form:	
	/*expr*/	create file from current line up to line containing *expr*. May be followed by ±n.
	%*expr*%	same as /*expr*/, no file creation
	line	create file from current line to *line*
	{*n*}	repeat previous argument *n* times

CT — Call Terminal and Start Login Process

% **ct** [*options*] *telnos*

Options:

– h	inhibit hangup
– s *speed*	set baud rate (**1200** default)
– v	send status information to **stderr**
– w *n*	wait up to *n* minutes for line
– x *n*	set debug level to *n* (0 to 9)

(continued)

CT, continued
    telnos   list of phone numbers to try

CTAGS — Create a Tags File of Functions and Typedefs
% **/usr/bin/ctags** [*options*] *sourcefiles*
% **/usr/xpg4/bin/ctags** [*options*] *sourcefiles*
Options:
– a	append output to existing tags file
– B	use backward searching pattern (?...?)
– f *file*	put tag descriptions in *file* (**tags** default)
– F	use forward searching pattern (/.../)
– t	create tags for typedefs
– u	update specified files in tags file
– v	produce function index on **stdout**
– w	suppress warnings
– x	print index of object names, line number, file name and line text on **stdout**

CU — Call UNIX System
% **cu** [*options*] *destination*
Options:
– b*n*	set character size to *n* bits (default is same as local terminal)
– c*type*	only use device matching *type*
– C	use command at end of command line
– d	print diagnostic traces
– e	set even parity
– h	simulate half duplex terminal
– H	ignore one hangup
– l*line*	line device name (default is first available)
– L	use /etc/uucp/System chat sequence
– n	prompt for telephone number
– o	set odd parity
– s*speed*	set baud rate (**any** default)
– t	set-up auto-answer ASCII terminal
destination	phone number, system name or LAN address

enter ~**?** to display the tilde command summary
enter ~**.** to exit **cu**

CUT — Cut Out Fields of File
% **cut – b***list* [**– n**] [*files*]
% **cut – c***list* [*files*]
% **cut – f***list* [**– d***char*] [**– s**] [*files*]
    stdin read if no *files* specified
Options:
– b*list*	pass specified byte positions
– c*list*	pass specified character positions
– d*c*	specify field delimiter (**tab** default)
– f*list*	pass specified fields
– n	do not split characters
– s	suppress lines with no delimiters
list	comma-separated list with optional – to indicate a range

CXREF — Produce C Cross Reference

% **cxref** [*options*] *files*

Options:

- **A***name* [(**def**)]
  associate *name* with *def* as if by **#assert**
- **A–**   forget predefined macros and assertions
- **c**   print combined cross reference
- **C**   only run first pass (create **.cx** file)
- **d**   disable printing declarations
- **D** *name* [=*def*]
  define *name* as *def* (**1** default)
- **F**   print full path of referenced files
- **I** *dir*   search *dir* before standard ones
- **l**   don't print local variables
- **L***n*   print in *n* columns (5 default)
- **o** *output* name of output file
- **s**   silent, don't print input filenames
- **t**   format output in columns of width 80
- **U** *symb* remove definition of *symb*
- **V**   print version information
- **w***n*   width of output is *n* (**80** default)
- **W***name,file,function,line*
  change width of at least 1 field
  from defaults:

name=15	*file*=13
function=15	*line*=20

Note: This is the 2.1 documentation for **cxref** as it is not included in the 2.5 documentation and may not be available in default command set.

DATE — Print Current Date

% **/usr/bin/date** [*option*] [+*format*]

% **/usr/xpg4/bindate** [*option*] [+*format*]

Option:

- **a**[-] [*s.f*] slowly adjust time by *s.f* seconds
- **u**   display date in GMT

format can be one or more of the following special characters:

%a	abbreviated weekday – **Sun** to **Sat**
%A	full weekday name
%b	abbreviated month name
%B	full month name
%c	locale's date and time format
%d	day – **01** to **31**
%D	date as *mm*/*dd*/*yy*
%e	day of month – **1** to **31**
%h	same as **%b**
%H	hour – **00** to **23**
%I	hour – **01** to **12**
%j	julian date – **001** to **366**
%m	month – **01** to **12**
%M	minute – **00** to **59**
%n	insert newline
%p	locale's **AM** or **PM** equivalent

(continued)

%r	time in AM/PM notation	
%R	time as *hh:mm* (24-hour)	
%S	second – **00** to **61**	
%t	insert tab character	
%T	time as *hh:mm:ss* (24-hour)	
%U	week number – **00** to **53** (Sun as first day)	
%w	day of week – Sun = **0**	
%W	week number – **00** to **53** (Mon first day)	
%x	locale's date format	
%X	locale's time format	
%y	last 2 digits of year – **00** to **99**	
%Y	4-digit year	
%Z	time zone name	

DC — Arbitrary Precision Desk Calculator
% **dc** [*file*]
> **stdin** read after *file*

DD — Convert and Copy File
% **dd** [*options*]
Options:

bs=*n*	both input and output block sizes	
cbs=*n*	conversion buffer size (logical record length)	
conv=	**ascii**	convert EBCDIC to ASCII
	block	convert to fixed length records
	ebcdic	convert ASCII to EBCDIC
	ibm	different ASCII to EBCDIC
	lcase	map upper case to lower
	noerror	continue on error
	notruncf	do not truncate output file
	swab	swap each pair of bytes
	sync	pad every record to value of **ibs**
	ucase	map lower case to upper
	unblock	convert to variable length records
	...,...	multiple conversions separated by commas
count=*n*	copy only *n* records	
files=*n*	number of input files to copy (tape)	
ibs=*n*	input block size (**512** default)	
if=*file*	input filename (**stdin** default)	
iseek=*n*	seek *n* input blocks (disk)	
obs=*n*	output block size (**512** default)	
of=*file*	output filename (**stdout** default)	
oseek=*n*	seek *n* output records	
seek=*n*	synonym for **oseek**	
skip=*n*	skip *n* input blocks (tape)	
n	number of bytes with optional suffix **k**, **b** or **w**; to specify multiplication by 1024, 512, 2 or a product indicated by two numbers separated by an **x**	

DELTA — Install a Change into SCCS Files
% **delta** [*options*] *files*
    SCCS filenames read from **stdin** if *files* is –
Options:

– g*list*	*list* of deltas to ignore
– m[*list*]	*list* of Modification Request numbers
– n	save edited file
– p	print delta differences in **diff** format
– r*sid*	specify SCCS ID of delta
– s	suppress printing of new SCCS ID, etc.
– y[*text*]	*text* inserted as comment

DEROFF — Remove Formatter Constructs
% **deroff** [*options*] [*files*]
    stdin read if no *files* specified
Options:

– i	ignore **.so** and **.nx** commands	
– m*x*	delete text from macro lines	
	l	for **mm** macros, delete **mm** lists
	m	for **mm** macros
	s	for **ms** macros
– w	build word list (1 word/line)	

DF — Report Free Block Count
% **df** [*options*] [*filesys*]
Options:

– b	print only k-bytes free
– e	print only files free
– F*type*	file system type (unmounted FSs)
– g	print entire **statvfs** structure
– i	display inode information
– k	print allocation in k-bytes
– l	report on local file systems only
– n	print only file system type
– o*opts*	specify file system type specific options
– t	print full listing with totals
– V	echo command; don't execute
filesys	list of file systems, directories and mounted resources

β **DF** — Report Free Block Count
% **df** [*options*] [*filesystems*] [*files*]
Options:

– a	report on all filesystems
– i	report number of used and free inodes
– t *type*	report on filesystems of specified type
filesystem	name of filesystem to report on
file	report on filesystem containing *file*

DIFF — Differential File Comparer

% **diff** [*options*] *file1 file2*
    stdin read if − specified for *file1* or *file2*
    valid options are **bitw** and one of **cCDefhn**

% **diff** [*options*] *dir1 dir2*
    compare files in specified directories
    valid options are **bilrsStw** and one of **cefhn**

Options:

− b	ignore trailing blanks, all whitespace equal
− c	list differences with 3 lines of context
− C *n*	same as **− c** with *n* lines
− D *str*	create merged version of *file1* and *file2* with C preprocessor controls; **#define** *str* equivalent to compiling *file2*
− e	produce **ed** script to make *file2* from *file1*
− f	produce script to make *file2* from *file1* (not **ed** compatible)
− h	do fast comparison (**− e** and **− f** not available)
− i	ignore case of letters
− l	produce long format output
− n	produce **ed** script to make *file1* from *file2* give count of changed lines
− r	recursive **diff** on subdirectories
− s	report identical files found
− S *file*	start directory diff at *file*
− t	expand TAB characters in output
− w	ignore all blanks, strings of blanks equivalent

Exit Status:

0	no differences
1	some differences
> 1	error

DIFF3 — Three Way File Compare

% **diff3** [*options*] *file1 file2 file3*

Options:

− 3	**ed** script for only lines with *file3* different
− e	**ed** script to add *file2* to *file3* changes to *file1*
− E	like **−e** but insert and flag overlapping changes
− x	**ed** script for only lines with all 3 files different
− X	like **−x** but insert and flag overlapping changes

DIFFMK — Mark Troff Input Differences

% **diffmk** *old new marked*

old	old version of file
new	new version of file
marked	generated file with change marks inserted

DIRCMP — Compare Two Directories
% **dircmp** [*options*] *dir1 dir2*
Options:

– d	compare files with same names, make list to make files in *dir2* like those in *dir1*
– s	don't print messages about identical files
– w*n*	width of output line is *n* chars (**72** default)

DIRNAME — Delete End of Pathname (See **BASENAME**)
% **dirname** *string*

DIS — Object Code Disassembler
% **/usr/ccs/bin/dis** [*options*] *files*
Options:

– C	display demangled C++ symbol names
– d *sect*	disassemble specified section, print offset of data from *sect* start
– D *sect*	disassemble specified section, print actual address of data
– F *function*	disassemble only *function*
– l *lib*	disassemble specified library (assumed to be in **LIBDIR**)
– o	print numbers in octal (hexadecimal default)
– t *sect*	disassemble *sect* as text
– V	print version information

DISPGID — Display All Valid Group IDs
% **dispgid**

DISPUID — Display All Valid User IDs
% **dispuid**

DOS2UNIX — Convert DOS Text files to ISO Format
% **dos2unix** [*option*] [*infile* [*outfile*]]
Options:

– 7	convert 8 bit DOS graphics characters to 7 bit characters
– ascii	remove extra CR's, convert DOS EOF character to Sun OS format
– iso	convert DOS extended character set to ISO (default)
infile	DOS file to convert (**stdin** read if no file specified)
outfile	converted file (**stdout** written if no file specified)

DOWNLOAD — Download PostScript Fonts
% **/usr/lib/lp/postscript/download** [*options*] [*files*]
Options:

– f	force complete scan of input file
– H *dir*	use *dir* as font directory (**/usr/lib/lp/postscript** default)

(continued)

DOWNLOAD, continued
  − m *name*   specify font map table
  − p *ptr*   first check resident font list
                /etc/lp/printers//*ptr*/**residentfonts**

DPOST — **troff** postprocessor for PostScript
% **dpost** [*options*] [*files*]
Options:
  − c *n*   print *n* copies of each page (**1** default)
  − e *lev*   set text encoding level (0, 1 or 2)
  − F *dir*   specify font directory
                (**/usr/lib/font** default)
  − H *dir*   specify host resident font directory
  − L *pro*   use *pro* as prologue
                (**/usr/lib/postscript/dpost.ps** default)
  − m *scale*   scale page by *scale* uniformly about
                origin (1.0 default)
  − n *n*   print *n* logical pages per physical page
  − o *list*   print only listed page numbers
  − O   disable picture inclusion
  − p l   print in landscape mode
  − p p   print in portrait mode (default)
  − T *name*   use font files for device *name*
                (**post** default)
  − w *n*   set width of line to *n* (**0.3** points default)
  − x *xoff*   origin offset; positive means right
                (**0** inches default)
  − y *yoff*   origin offset; positive means up
                (**0** inches default)

  list   comma-separated, *n* − *m* means range,
          − *n* means beginning to page *n*, *n* − means
          from page *n* to end
Note: the origin is near the upper left corner of the page.

DU — Summarize Disk Usage
% **du** [*options*] [*directories*]
Options:
  − a   generate entry for each file
          (directories only default)
  − s   display only a grand total summary

DUMP — Dump Object File or Archive Parts
% **dump** [*options*] *files*
Options: format: *option* [*modifiers*]
  − a   dump archive header of members
  − c   dump string table
  − C   dump decoded C++ symbol names
  − D   dump debug information
  − f   dump *file* headers
  − g   dump global symbols
  − h   dump section headers
  − l   dump line number information
  − L   dump dynamic linking and shared lib info
  − o   dump program execution header
  − r   dump relocation information
  − s   dump section contents in hex

(continued)

DUMP, continued

−t	dump symbol table
−Tx1[,x2]	dump symbol table entries specified by index x1 or range from x1 to x2
−V	print version information

Option Modifiers:

−d	m[,n]	dump section m or range m to n
−n	name	dump info related to name (with **hrst**)
−p		don't print headers
−v		symbolic dump

DUMPCS — Show Codeset Table for the Current Locale
% **dumpcs** [options]

−0	ASCII (EUC primary)
−1	EUC codeset 1, if used for locale
−2	EUC codeset 2, if used for locale
−3	EUC codeset 3, if used for locale
−v	verbose
−w	show corresponding wide character code values

DUMPKEYS — Dump Keyboard Translation Table
% **dumpkeys**

ECHO — Echo Arguments
$\kappa\sigma$ % **/usr/bin/echo** [strs]
ξ % **/usr/ucb/echo** [-n] [args]
% **echo** [strs]

-n	print without newline

Note: special escape conventions (place string in quotes)

\0n	character whose octal value is n n must be 3 digits if followed by other digits
\b	backspace
\c	print line without newline
\f	form feed
\n	newline
\r	carriage return
\t	tab
\v	vertical tab
****	backslash
strs	some strings to be echoed
args	arguments to be echoed

ED — Text Editor
% **ed** [options] [file]
See Page 2 for list of commands
Options:

−C		work with encrypted file (simulate C cmd)
−p	string	specify prompt string
−s		suppress counts, diagnostics, etc.
−x		work with encrypted file (simulate X cmd)

EDIT — Line Text Editor
% **/usr/bin/edit** [*options*] [*files*]
% **/usr/xpg4/bin/edit** [*options*] [*files*]
Options:

+ *cmd* | **-c** *cmd*	execute *cmd* at beginning of edit session
-C	work with encrypted file (simulate C cmd)
-l	set up for editing LISP programs
-L	list files saved after crash
-r *file*	recover file after crash
-R	readonly mode
-	suppress interactive feedback; for processing editor scripts
-s	suppress interactive feedback; for processing editor scripts
-t *tag*	edit file containing *tag*
-v *n*	evoke vi
-V *n*	verbose
-w *n*	default window size to *n*
-x	work with encrypted file (simulate X cmd)

EGREP — Search File for Pattern (See **GREP**)
% **/usr/bin/egrep** [*options*] [*expr*] [*files*]
% **/usr/xpg4/bin/egrep** [*options*] [*expr*] [*files*]
   stdin read if no *files* specified
Options:

-b	precede line with block number
-c	print count of matching lines only
-e *expr*	useful if the expression starts with a –
-f *file*	take expression from *file*
-h	don't print filenames
-i	ignore case
-l	print only names of files with matching lines
-n	print line numbers
-s	silent
-v	print non-matching lines
-x	match entire lines only

See Page 173 for Regular Expressions
Exit Status:

0	match(es) found
1	no match found
2	syntax error or inaccessible files

EJECT — Eject Media from Drive
% **eject** [*options*] [*device*]
Options:

-d	display default device name
-f	eject even if busy
-n	display "nickname" translation table
-q	query if media present
device	device name or "nickname"

(continued)

41

EJECT, continued

Exit Status:

0	successful (media in drive with **– q**)
1	fail (media not in drive with **– q**)
2	invalid flags
3	**ioctl()** call failed
4	ready on manual eject media

ENV — Alter Environment and Execute Command

% **env** [*options*] [*command* [*args*]]

% **env**

    print current environment variables

Options:

– i	set environment only to specified values
–	set environment only to specified values
name = *value*	
	set environment variable *name* to *value*
args	passed to *command*

EQN — Typeset Mathematics

% **eqn** [*options*] [*files*]

    stdin read if no *files* specified

Options:

– dxy	set equation delimiters to x and y
– fn	global change to font n
– pn	reduce subscript and superscript size by n points (**3** default)
– sn	set global point size to n

ERRDATE — Provide Diagnostic for Invalid Date

% **/usr/sadm/bin/errdate** [*options*]

(see also **ckdate**)

Options:

– e *errmsg*	set error message to *errmsg*	
– f *fmt*	input format:	
	%b	abbreviated month name
	%B	full month name
	%d	day of month (01-31)
	%D	date as %m/%d/%y (default)
	%e	day of month (1-31)
	%h	same as **%b%**
	%m	month number (01-12)
	%y	year within century
	%Y	year (4 digits)
– W *width*	format messages to *width* characters	

ERRGID — Provide Diagnostic for Invalid Group Id

% **/usr/sadm/bin/errgid** [*options*]

(see also **ckgid**)

Options:

– e *errmsg*	set error message to *errmsg*
– W *width*	format messages to *width* characters

ERRINT — Provide Diagnostic for Invalid Integers
% **/usr/sadm/bin/errint** [*options*]
(see also **ckint**)
Options:
- **−b** *base*   numeric base (2-36, **10** default)
- **−e** *errmsg* set error message to *errmsg*
- **−W** *width* format messages to *width* characters

ERRITEM — Provide Diagnostic for Invalid Menu Items
% **/usr/sadm/bin/erritem** [*options*] [*choices*]
(see also **ckitem**)
Options:
- **−e** *errmsg* set error message to *errmsg*
- **−W** *width* format messages to *width* characters

choice a menu line item

ERRPATH — Provide Diagnostic for Invalid Pathnames
% **/usr/sadm/bin/errpath** [*options*]
(see also **ckpath**)
Options:
- **−a**   must be absolute
- **−b**   pathname must be block special file
- **−c**   pathname must be character special file
- **−e** *errmsg* set error message to *errmsg*
- **−f**   pathname must be regular file
- **−l**   pathname must be relative
- **−n**   pathname must not exist
- **−o**   pathname must exist
- **−r**   pathname must be readable
- **−t**   pathname must be touchable
- **−w**   pathname must be writable
- **−W** *width* format messages to *width* characters
- **−x**   pathname must be executable
- **−y**   pathname must be directory
- **−z**   pathname must be non-zero size file

ERRANGE — Provide Diagnostic for Invalid Integer
     Ranges
% **/usr/sadm/bin/errange** [*options*]
(see also **ckrange**)
Options:
- **−b** *base*   numeric base (**2-36**, **10** default)
- **−e** *errmsg*
             set error message to *errmsg*
- **−l** *low*   lower limit of range
- **−u** *high*   upper limit of range
- **−W** *width* format messages to *width* characters

ERRSTR — Provide Diagnostic for Invalid Strings
% **/usr/sadm/bin/errstr** [*options*]
(see also **ckstr**)
Options:
- **−e** *errmsg* set error message to *errmsg*
- **−l** *len*   maximum length of input

(continued)

ERRSTR, continued

> **−r** *regexp* match regular expression with input
> (multiple permitted; input only need
> match one)
> **−W** *width* format messages to *width* characters

ERRTIME — Provide Diagnostic for Invalid Time
% **/usr/sadm/bin/errtime** [*options*]
(see also **cktime**)
Options:

> **−e** *errmsg* set error message to *errmsg*
> **−f** *fmt* input format:
>
> | | |
> |---|---|
> | **%H** | hour (00-23) |
> | **%I** | hour (00-12) |
> | **%M** | minute (00-59) |
> | **%p** | AM or PM |
> | **%r** | time as **%I:%M:%S %p** |
> | **%R** | time as **%H:%M** (default) |
> | **%S** | seconds (00-59) |
> | **%T** | time as **%H:%M:%S** |
>
> **−W** *width* format messages to *width* characters

ERRUID — Provide Diagnostic for Invalid User ID
% **/usr/sadm/bin/erruid** [*options*]
(see also **ckuid**)
Options:

> **−e** *errmsg* set error message to *errmsg*
> **−W** *width* format messages to *width* characters

ERRYORN — Provide Diagnostic for Invalid Yes/No
% **/usr/sadm/bin/erryorn** [*options*]
(see also **ckyorn**)
Options:

> **−e** *errmsg* set error message to *errmsg*
> **−W** *width* format messages to *width* characters

β **ERROR** — Insert Compiler Errors With Source Lines
% **error** [*options*] [*file*]
> run with stdin piped to error message source
Options:

> **−n** all messages sent to stdout; no files
> touched
> **−q** error opts for file to be touched
> **−s** print error categorization statistics
> **−t***suflst* files not in *suflst* not touched
> **−v** load touched files positioned into vi

ξκσ **EVAL** — Evaluate Expressions
% **eval** [*args*]

EX — Text Editor
% **/usr/bin/ex** [*options*] [*files*]
% **/usr/xpg4/bin/ex** [*options*] [*files*]
Options:

+ *cmd*	execute *cmd* at beginning of edit session
−c *cmd*	execute *cmd* at beginning of edit session
−C	work with encrypted file (simulate C cmd)
−l	set up for editing LISP programs
−L	list filenames of files saved in crash
−r *file*	retrieve last saved version of named file after system or editor crash
−R	set **readonly** option
-	suppress interactive feedback; for processing editor scripts
−s	suppress interactive feedback; for processing editor scripts
−t *tag*	edit file containing *tag* and position editor at its definition
−v	equivalent to using **vi**
−V	verbose
−w*n*	set window size to *n*
−x	work with encrypted file (simulate X cmd)

ξ **EXEC** — Execute Commands from Shell
% **exec** *command*

κσ **EXEC** — Execute Commands from Shell
% **exec** [*args*]

ξ **EXIT** — Exit Shell
% **exit** [(*expression*)]

κσ **EXIT** — Exit Shell
% **exit** [*n*]
n   return value to relay

EXPAND — Expand Tabs to Spaces
% **expand** [*option*] [*files*]
Options:

−*n*	establish tabs every *n* characters
−*tablist*	comma-delimited list of tab locations
−t *tablst*	tab stops separated by whitespace or commas

κ **EXPORT** — Create Environment or Global Variable Access
% **export** *defs*

defs[*var* [**=***val*]]
var   variable to be exported
val   value of variable

σ EXPORT — Create Environment or Global Variable Access
% **export** [*var*]

var   existing variable to be exported

EXPR — Evaluate Expression Arguments
% **expr** *args*

β EXPR — Evaluate Expression Arguments
% **/usr/ucb/expr** *args*

Binary operators:

\l	return first operand if first is not null or 0
\&	return first operand if neither is null or 0
=, \>, \>=, \<, \<=, !=	
	integer comparison operators
+, -, *, /, %	
	integer arithmetic operators
:	match operator - returns number of bytes matched or use \(. . . \) to return portion of first operand. (second *arg* must be regular expression)

index *str char-seq*
> return first position in *str* where any *char* in *char-seq* matches

length *str*   return length of string
match *exp1 expr2*
> same as :
substr *str index cnt*
> return *cnt* characters of *str* starting at *index*

Note: regular expressions are as in **ed** except all patterns are anchored so ^ is not a special character.

Exit Status:

0	expression is neither null nor 0
1	expression is null or 0
2	expression is invalid
>2	error

EXSTR — Extract Strings from C Source
% **exstr** [*options*] *files*
Options:

–d	at run time, print message if **gettxt()** fails
–e	include position information in extraction
–r	replace strings with calls to **gettxt()**

φ FACE — Framed Access Command Environment
% **face** [*options*] [*files*]
Options:

–a	*afile*	specify alias file
–c	*cfile*	modify FMLI commands with *cfile*
–i	*ifile*	specify initialization file

(continued)

FACE, continued

file is a full pathname for file describing object being opened initially;
if no *files* specified, opens objects specified
by **LOGINWIN** environment variable from **.environ** file.

Naming convention:

Menu.*xxx*	menu
Form.*xxx*	form
Text.*xxx*	text file

FACTOR — Print Prime Factors of a Number
% **factor** [*n*]

n	**stdin** read if *n* not specified

FALSE — Return Unsuccessful Exit Status (See **TRUE**)
% **false**

FC — Process Command Histories
% **/usr/bin/fc** [*first* [*last*]]
% **/usr/bin/fc** -**l** [-**nr**] [*first* [*last*]]
% **/usr/bin/fc** -**s** [*old*=*new*] [*first*]
Options:

− **l**	list commands
− **n**	suppress command numbers when using -**l**
− **r**	reverse order of listing
− **s**	re-execute without evoking editor

cmd   any entry in the history file
first and *last* may be as follows:

[+]*n*	positive integer indicating the command number, which is the number of the command in the history file
-*n*	negative integer indicating the number of times ago the command was executed
str	most recent command beginning with string *str*

new   substring to substite for *old*
old   substring to be object of substitution

κ **FC** — Process Command Histories
% **fc** -**e** [*old*=*new*] [*cmd*]
Options:

− **e**	re-execute without evoking editor
− **l**	list commands
− **n**	suppress command numbers when using -**l**
− **r**	reverse order of listing

cmd   any entry in the history file
first and *last* may be as follows:

[+]*n*	positive integer indicating the command number, which is the number of the command in the history file

(continued)

FC, continued

-*n*	negative integer indicating the number of times ago the command was executed
str	most recent command beginning with string *str*
new	substring to substite for *old*
old	substring to be object of substitution

FDFORMAT — Format Floppy Disks

% **fdformat** [*options*] [*device*]

Options:

– b *label*	put MS-DOS label on disk
– B	install boot loader in *file*
– d	MS-DOS format
– D	force double density (720 Kb)
– e	eject diskette when done
– E	force extended density (2.88 Mb)
– f	don't confirm before formatting
– H	force high density (1.2 Mb or 1.44 Mb)
– l	same as **– D**
– L	same as **– D**
– m	medium density (1200k); with **– t nec** only
– M	same as **-m**
– q	don't print status messages
– t dos	MS-DOS format
– t nec	NEC-DOS format
– U	unmount prior to formatting
– v	verify after formatting
– x	write SunOS label or MS-DOS format, skipping further processing

ξκσ FG — Resume Execution in Foreground

See **Job Control** in Solaris SHELL section Pages 168-172

FGREP — Search File for Pattern (See GREP)

% **/usr/bin/fgrep** [*options*] [*string*] [*files*]

% **/usr/xpg4/bin/fgrep** [*options*] [*string*] [*files*]

    stdin read if no *files* specified

Options:

– b	precede line with block number
– c	print count of matching lines only
– e *expr*	useful if expression starts with a **–**
– f *file*	take *strings* from *file*
– h	suppress print of filenames
– i	ignore case of letters
– l	print only names of files with matching lines
– n	print line numbers
– s	silent, only print error messages
– v	print non-matching lines
– x	print exact matches (whole line) only

Exit Status:

0	match(es) found
1	no match found
2	error

FILE — Attempt to Classify Files
% **file** [*option*] *files*
% **/usr/ucb/file** [*option*] *files*
Option:

– c	check magic file for format errors,
– f *nfile*	use *nfile* as a file of filenames
– L	same as **h**
– m *magic*	use alternate magic file (**/etc/magic** default)

FIND — Find Files
% **find** *pathname-list expression*

pathname-list	directories where search is to begin
expression	formed from one or more primaries

Primaries:

– atime *n*	true if file found was accessed *n* days ago
– cpio *dev*	write file on *dev* in cpio format (5120 byte records)
– ctime *n*	true if file found was changed *n* days ago
– depth	always true; causes entries in directory to be acted on before the directory itself
– exec *cmd*	execute *cmd*, true if successful exit status; replace {} by current pathname; command must end with a ;
– follow	always true; follow symbolic links
– fstype *type*	true if file in filesystem of specified type
– group *name*	true if file found is owned by the group *name*
– inum *n*	true if file has inode number *n*
– links *n*	true if file found has *n* links
– local	true if file is on local system
– ls	always true; print current pathname with statistics
– mount	don't cross mounted file systems, always true
– mtime *n*	true if file found was modified *n* days ago
– name *pat*	true if *pat* matches name of file found
– ncpio *dev*	write file on *dev* in -c cpio format (5120 byte records)
– newer *file*	true if file found modified after *file*
– nogroup	true if file group not in group file
– nouser	true if file owner not in password file
– ok *cmd*	like **– exec** except user prompted first
– perm [–]*octal*	true if permission of file found is *octal* – forces true if any bits in *octal* match a file permission
– print	print name of files found, always true
– prune	do not continue down tree

(continued)

FIND, continued

- **-size** *n*[**c**]   true if file found is *n* blocks [characters]
  long
- **-type** *c*   true if file found is:

b	block special file
c	character special file
d	directory
f	plain file
l	symbolic link
p	fifo or named pipe

- **-user** *name*

       true if file found is owned by user or
  ID *name*
- \(*expr* \)   true if *expr* is true, used for grouping

- *n*   *n* means exactly *n*, +*n* means more than *n*
       −*n* means less than *n*

Ways to join primaries:
- ! *expr*   negate truth value of *expr*
- *exp1* [**-a**] *exp2*
       true if both *exp1* and *exp2* are true
- *exp1* **-o** *exp2*
       true if either *exp1* or *exp2* is true

FINGER — Find Information about Users
% **finger** [*options*] [*users*]
% **finger** [**-l**] *rusers*
Options:

-b	in-between size output format
-f	suppress header
-h	suppress printing **.project** file
-i	just show idle time for *users*
-l	long output format
-m	match *user* to login name only
-p	don't show information from **.plan** file
-q	quick list of users
-s	short output format
-w	like **-s** but don't show full name

rusers   remote users of form *name*@*host*

φ FMLCUT — Cut Out Fields of File
% **fmlcut** **-c**list [*files*]
% **fmlcut** **-f**list [**-d**char] [**-s**] [*files*]
    stdin read if no *files* specified
Options:

-clist	pass specified character positions
-dc	specify field delimiter (**tab** default)
-flist	pass specified fields
-s	suppress lines with no delimiters
list	comma-separated list with optional − to indicate a range

Exit Status:

0	successful
2	syntax error

φ **FMLEXPR** — Evaluate Expression Arguments
% **fmlexpr** *args*
Binary operators:

|	return first operand if first is not null or 0
\&	return first operand if neither is null or 0
=, \>, \>=, \<, \<=, !=	
	integer comparison operators
+, −, *, /, %	
	integer arithmetic operators
:	match operator - returns number of bytes matched or use \(. . . \) to return portion of first operand. (second *arg* must be regular expression)
index *str char-seq*	
	return first position in *str* where any *char* in *char-seq* matches
length *str*	return length of string
match *exp1 expr2*	
	same as :
substr *str index cnt*	
	return *cnt* characters of *str* starting at *index*

Note: regular expressions are as in **ed** except all patterns are anchored so ˆ is not a special character.

Exit Status:

0	expression is neither null nor 0
1	expression is null or 0
2	expression is invalid

φ **FMLGREP** — Search File for Pattern
% **fmlgrep** [*options*] [*string*] [*files*]
    stdin read if no *files* specified
Options:

− b	precede line with block number
− c	print count of matching lines only
− i	ignore case of letters
− l	print only names of files with matching lines
− n	print line numbers
− s	silent, only print error messages
− v	print non-matching lines

Exit Staus:

0	match(es) found
1	no match found
2	error

φ **FMLI** — Form and Menu Language Interpreter
% **fmli** [*options*] *files*
Options:

− a *alias*	name of alias file containing *alias=pathname* lines
− c *cfile*	modify FMLI commands with *cfile*

(continued)

FMLI, continued
  – i *init*   initialization file specifying characteristics
             of application including transient
             introductory frame, banner, color
             attributes and Screen Labeled Keys (SLK)

FMT — Simple Text Formatter
% **fmt** [*options*] *files*
Options:
  – c   crown margin mode; preserve
             indentation of first two lines, align
             to second line
  – s   split only; don't join short lines
  – w *n*   fill output up to *n* columns

FMTMSG — Display Message on **stderr** or Console
% **fmtmsg** [*options*] *text*
Options:
  – a *action* "to fix" description
  – c *class*   source of message
             firm   firmware condition
             hard   hardware condition
             soft   software condition
  – l *from*   source of the message
  – s *severity* seriousness of error
             error   fault detected
             halt   fatal error
             info   information only; not error
             warn   abnormal condition
  – t *tag*   message identifier
  – u *subclass*
             comma-separated list from below:
             appl   condition originated in application
             console write message to console
             nrecov application will not recover
             opsys   condition originated in kernel
             print   print message to **stderr**
             recov   application will recover
             util   condition originated in utility
  text   text string describing condition (write so it
             appears as a single argument to program)

Exit Status:
  0   no severity indicated
  1   halt
  2   error
  3   warning
  4   info

FNATTR — Access/Modify FNS Named Object Attributes
% **fnattr** [**-admls**] *nam* [**-O** | **-U**] *id* [**vals**]
Options:
  – a   add an attribute or add
             a value to an attribute
  – d   delete attributes

(continued)

FNATTR, continued

	−l	list attributes
	−m	modify attribute values
	−s	add in supersede mode
	−O	format of *id* is FN_ID_ISO_OID_STRING, an ASN.1 dot-separated integer list string
	−U	format of *id* is FN_ID_DCE_UUID, a DCE UUID in string form
nam		name for reference
id		identifier of attributes
vals		attribute values

FNBIND — Bind Reference to an FNS Name
% **fnbind** [-**svL**] *nam nwnam*
% **fnbind** [-**rsv**] *nwnam* [-**O** | -**U**] *reftyp* [-**O** | -**U**]
　　adrtyp [-**c** | -**x**] *adrcont*
Options:

	−c	store *adrcont* in existing form; don't use XDR-encoding
	−O	ID format is FN_ID_ISO_OID_STRING, an ASN.1 dot-separated integer list string
	−r	create a reference
	−s	bind to *nwnam*
	−U	identifier format is FN_ID_DCE_UUID, a DCE UUID in string form
	−v	display the reference being bound to *nwnam*
	−x	change *adrcont* to hex and store; no XDR-encoding
nam		name for reference
nwnam		new name for reference
reftyp		reference type
adrtyp		address type
adcont		address contents

FNLIST — Display Names and References Bound in FNS
% **fnlist** [*options*] *compnam*
Options:

	−l	show references and names bound in context of *compnam*
	−v	verbose
compnam		composite name

FNLOOKUP — Display Reference Bound to FNS Name
% **fnlookup** [*options*] *compnam*
Options:

	−v	verbose
	−L	show references bound to an XFN link
compnam		composite name

FNRENAME — Rename Binding of FNS name
% **fnrename** [*options*] *contnam old_atname new_atname*
Options:

– s	show references and names bound in context of *compnam*
– v	verbose

contnam	context name
old_atname	old atomic name
new_atname	new atomic name

FNUNBIND — Bind Reference to an FNS Name
% **fnunbind** *compnam*

compnam	composite name

FOLD — Fold Long Lines
% **fold** [*option*] *files*
stdin read if no *files* specified
Options:

- w *n*	fold to *n* columns (80 default)
– *n*	fold to *n* columns (80 default)
– b	count width in bytes instead of columns
– s	segment if blanks allow

κσ **FOR** — Shell For-Loop Function
% **for** *word* [**in** *wordlist...*] ; **do** *cmds* ; **done**

word	something that returns a value to be compared
wordlist	some list of strings; may be generated from a directory spec or a variable
cmds	valid Solaris, Solaris shell or KornShell commands

ξ **FOREACH** — Shell For-Loop Function
% **foreach** *word* **(** *wordlist* **)**
    cmds
    end

cmds	a valid Solaris or C shell command

β **FROM** — Display Email Sender and Date
% **/usr/ucb/from** [*option*] *user*
stdin read if no *files* specified
Options:

– s *sender*	only mail from *sender*

FTP — File Transfer Program
% **ftp** [*options*] [*hostname*]
Options:

– d	enable debugging
– g	disable filename expansion
– i	disable interactive prompting during multi-file transfers
– n	disable auto-login
– t	enable packet tracing (ignored)

(continued)

FTP, continued

   – v   show all remote responses
                  (default if interactive)

If local filename (*lfile*) is **–**, **stdin** or **stdin** is used;
if first character of *lfile* is |, command is piped
to remainder of command line.

FTP Commands

   ! [*cmd*]   run *cmd* on local machine
                  if no *cmd*, spawn interactive shell
   $ *mac* [*args*]
                  execute macro *mac* w/optional *args*
   account [*passwd*]
                  supply supplemental password
   ? [*cmd*]   same as **help**
   append   *lfile* [*rfile*]
                  append *lfile* to *rfile*
   ascii   set representation type to network ASCII
   bell   sound bell after each file transfer
   binary   set representation type to image
   bye   terminate session with remote and
                  exit **ftp**
   case   toggle case mapping (off default)
   cd *rdir*   change to *rdir* on remote system
   cdup   move "up" one directory on remote
   close   terminate session with remote; return to
                  command interpreter
   cr   toggle <cr> stripping during ASCII
                  retrieval
   delete *rfile*
                  delete *rfile* on remote system
   debug   toggle debugging mode
   dir [*rdir*] [*lfile*]
                  list remote directory contents; optionally
                  put output in *lfile*
   disconnect
                  same as **close**
   form [*format*]
                  set carriage control format subtype
   get *rfile* [*lfile*]
                  retrieve *rfile*; store on local system
   glob   toggle file name expansion
   hash   toggle # display for each block transferred
   help [*cmd*] get help with *cmd*;
                  if no *args*, print command summary
   lcd [*dir*]   change directory on local system
                  (**$HOME** default)
   ls [*rdir*] [*lfile*]
                  short directory listing on remote system;
                  output to *lfile* (terminal default)
   macdef *mname*
                  all input until blank line becomes
                  definition of macro *mname*
                  use **$***n* to refer to parameters
                  use **$i** to loop through parameters
   mdelete [*rfiles*]
                  delete *rfiles* on remote system

(continued)

FTP, continued

mdir *rfiles file*
    multi-file **dir**; output to *file*

mget *rfiles*
    get multiple files from remote system

mkdir *rdir* make directory on remote system

mls *rfiles lfile*
    multi-file **ls**

mode [**stream**]
    set transfer mode to **stream**

mput *files* expand wild cards and execute **put**
    for each file

nmap [*in out*]
    set filename mapping;
    if no arguments, unset

ntrans [*in* [*out*]]
    set the filename character translation:
    if no arguments, unset

open *host* [*port*]
    connect to *host*; optional port number
    may be supplied

prompt toggle interactive prompting during
    mdelete, mget, mput

proxy *ftp_cmd*
    execute ftp command on secondary
    connection

put *lfile* [*rfile*]
    store local file on remote machine
    (*rfile* defaults to "mapped" *lfile*)

pwd print current directory name on remote

quit same as **bye**

quote *arg1 arg2*
    send args to remote server

recv *rfile* [*lfile*]
    same as **get**

remotehelp [*cmd*]
    get help from remote server

rename *file1 file2*
    rename *file1* as *file2* on remote

reset clear reply queue

rmdir *rdir* remove directory on remote system

runique toggle local unique filename mapping

send *lfile* [*rfile*]
    same as **put**

sendport toggle use of PORT commands

status show current status of ftp

struct [**file**]
    set file structure

sunique toggle remote unique filename mapping

tenex set to talk to TENEX systems

trace toggle packet tracing (unimplemented)

type [*type*] set representation type: **ascii**,
    binary, **image** (**ascii** default)

user *name* [*passwd*] [*accnt*]
    sign on to remote server

verbose toggle verbose mode

κ FUNCTION — Define a KornShell Function
% **function** *identifier* { *list* ;}
% *identifier*() { *list* ;}

GCORE — Get Core Image of Processes
% **gcore** [*option*] [*pids*]
Option:

– o *file*	core images to *file.pid*	
	(**core**.*pid* default)	
– p *procdir*	not in Solaris 2.5 manual	

GENCAT — Generate Formatted Message Catalog
% **gencat** *cfile mfiles*

cfile	catalog file to be created
mfiles	files of messages to catalog

GET — Retrieve an SCCS File Version
% **get** [*options*] *files*
    SCCS filenames read from **stdin** if *files* is –
Options:

– an	specify delta sequence number retrieved
– b	create new branch (**– e** required)
– cwhen	do not include deltas made after *when*
	(format: *YY* [*MM* [*DD* [*HH* [*MM* [*SS*]]]]])
– e	retrieve the version for editing
– g	suppress version retrieval
– Gname	use *name* as retrieved
	version
– ilist	*list* of deltas to include;
	list is comma-delimited or – range
– k	SCCS ID keywords not replaced
– l	delta summary written to **l**.*file*
– lp	delta summary written to **stdout**
– m	precede each line with related SCCS ID
– n	precede each line with %**M**% ID keyword
– p	retrieved version written to **stdout**
– rsid	specify SCCS ID of version
– s	suppress **stdout** output
– t	access most recent delta of release or
	release and level
– xlist	*list* of deltas to exclude;
	list is comma delimited or – range

GETCONF — Get Configuration Values
% **getconf** *sysvar*
% **getconf** *pathvar pathname*

sysvar	system environment variable
pathvar	system environment variable holding
	path names
pathname	path names

GETFACL — Get ACL Information for Files
% **getfacl** [*options files*
Options:

– a	display filename, owner, group and ACL
– d	display filename, owner, group and default ACL (if exists)

Format of ACL:
#file:filename
#owner:uid
#group:gid
user::perm
user:uid:perm
group::perm
group:gid:perm
mask::perm
other::perm
default:user::perm
default:user:uid:perm
default:group::perm
default:group:gid:perm
default:mask:perm
default:other:perm

φ **GETFRM** — Get FMLI Frame ID
% **getfrm**

φ **GETITEMS** — Get List of Marked Menu Items
% **getitems** [*delim*]
returns **lininfo** if undefined, else value of
the **name** descriptor

delim   delimiter string for returned string

GETOPT — Parse Command Options
(being replaced by **getopts**)
% **set – –** '**getopt** *string* **$ * '**

string   list of recognized option letters

GETOPTCVT — Convert From **getopt** to **getopts**
% **/usr/lib/getoptcvt** [*option*] [*file*]
Option:

   – b   make backward compatible script

GETOPTS — Parse Command Options
% **/usr/bin/getopts** *string var* [*args*]

args	parse *args*
var	shell variable to place next option in
string	list of recognized option letters; followed by **:** if option has argument

GETTEXT — Get String from Message Database
% **gettext***txtdom***:***msgid*

(continued)

GETTEXT, continued
txtdom   text domain
msgid   message identifier

GETTXT — Get String from Message Database
% **gettxt** *mfile*:*mnum* [*dflt_msg*]

mfile   file in **/usr/lib/locale/***locale***/LC_MESSAGES**
           to retrieve string from
mnum   sequence number of string to get from *msgfile*
dflt_msg default string to display on failure

ξ **GLOB** — Expand Wordlist
% **glob** [*wordlist*]

ξ **GOTO** — Branch Out of Code Sequence
% **goto** [*label*]
label   identifier indicating point to branch to

GPROF — Display Call-Graph Profile Data
% **gprof** [*options*] [*imgfile*] [*proffile*] [-*n nfs*]
Options:

−a	suppress print of statically declared functions
−b	brief
−c	discover static call-graphs of program
−C	demangle C++ symbol names before printing
−D	produce a differences profile file
−e *fn-name*	suppress information for specified functions and their descendents
−E *fn-name*	provide abbreviated information for specified function
−f *fn-name*	print graph entry only for specified function and its descendents
−F *fn-name*	print graph entry only for specified function and its descendents
−l	suppress print of graph profile entries for local symbols
−nnfs	limits size of flat and graph profile listings to top *nfs*
−s	print summation file gmon.sum entries for local symbols
−z	print routines with zero usage

fn-name function name
imgfile image file
proffile profile file

GRAPH -
% **graph** [*options*]
Options:

−a *spacing* [*start*]		
	supply abscissaes automatically	
−b	break graph after each label	
	in input	
−c *string*	*string* is default label for each point	
−g *gridstyle*		
	gridstyle is 0 for no grid,	
	1 frame with ticks, 2 full grid	
−h *frac*	fraction of space for height	
−l *label*	label for graph	
−m *connectmode*		
	mode of connecting lines:	
	0 disconnected, 1 connected (default);	
	some devices have other specifiable line	
	styles	
−r *frac*	fraction of space to move right before	
	plotting	
−s	Save screen, do not erase before	
	plotting	
−t	transpose axes; **-x** applies to vertical	
	axis	
−u *frac*	fraction of space to move up before	
	plotting	
−w *frac*	fraction of space for width	
−x [**1**] *lower* [*upper* [*spacing*]]		
	x axis specifications	
−y [**1**] *lower* [*upper* [*spacing*]]		
	y axis specifications	

GREP — Search File for Pattern (See **EGREP**, **FGREP**)
% **/usr/bin/grep** [*options*] *pattern* [*files*]
% **/usr/xpg4/bin/grep** [*options*] *pattern* [*files*]
    stdin read if no *files* specified
(See Page 173 for Regular Expressions)
Options:

−b	precede line with block number
	(0 is first block)
−c	print count of matching lines only
−e *exp*	search for regexp that begins with −
−f *file*	use list of regexp from *file*
−h	don't print filenames
−h	suppress print of filenames
−i	ignore case of letters in comparisons
−l	print only names of files with
	matching lines
−n	print line numbers
−s	suppress file error messages
−v	print non-matching lines
−w	search for *pattern* as a "word"

(continued)

GREP, continued
Exit Staus:

0	match(es) found
1	no match found
2	syntax errors or inaccessible files (including when matches are found)

GROUPS — Display Group Membership of User
% **groups** [*users*]

β **GROUPS** — Display Group Membership of User
% **/usr/ucb/groups** [*users*]

GRPCK — Validate Group File
% **/usr/etc/grpck** [*file*]
/etc/group read if no *file* specified

HASH — Evaluate Directory Contents Hash Tables
% **/usr/bin/hash** [*utility*]
% **/usr/bin/hash** [**-r**]
Option:
    – r   forget all remembered locations

κ **HASH** — Evaluate Directory Contents Hash Tables
% **hash** [*names*]

σ **HASH** — Evaluate Directory Contents Hash Tables
% **hash** [**-r**] [*names*]
Option:
    – r   forget all remembered locations

ξ **HASHSTAT** — Evaluate Directory Contents Hash Tables
% **hashstat**

HEAD — Print First Lines of File
% **head** [*option*] [*files*]
  stdin read if no *files* specified
Option:
    – *num*   print the first *num* lines
    – n *num* print the first *num* lines

HELP — Explain a Message or SCCS Command
% **help** [*args*]
    args   **sccs** commands or message numbers
    help stuck display info on using **help**

HELPDATE — Provide Help Text for Date
% **/usr/sadm/bin/helpdate** [*options*]
(see also **ckdate**)
Options:
    – f *fmt*   input format:
            %b   abbreviated month name
            %B   full month name
            %d   day of month (01-31)
            %D   date as %m/%d/%y (default)
            %e   day of month (1-31)

(continued)

HELPDATE, continued

	%h	same as **%b%**
	%m	month number (01-12)
	%y	year within century
	%Y	year (4 digits)

    – h *hlpmsg* set help message to *hlpmsg*
    – W *width* format messages to *width* characters

HELPGID — Provide Help Text for Group ID
% **/usr/sadm/bin/helpgid** [*options*]
(see also **ckgid**)
Options:
    – h *hlpmsg* set help message to *hlpmsg*
    – m display list of groups as help or
               error response
    – W *width* format messages to *width* characters

HELPINT — Provide Help Text for Integer
% **/usr/sadm/bin/helpint** [*options*]
(see also **ckint**)
Options:
    – b *base* numeric base (2-36, **10** default)
    – h *hlpmsg* set help message to *hlpmsg*
    – W *width* format messages to *width* characters

HELPITEM — Provide Help Text for Menu Item
% **/usr/sadm/bin/helpitem** [*options*] [*choices*]
(see also **ckitem**)
Options:
    – h *hlpmsg* set help message to *hlpmsg*
    – W *width* format messages to *width* characters

choice   a menu line item

HELPPATH — Provide Help Text for Pathname
% **/usr/sadm/bin/helppath** [*options*]
(see also **ckpath**)
Options:
    – a pathname must be absolute
    – b pathname must be block special file
    – c pathname must be character special file
    – f pathname must be regular file
    – h *hlpmsg* set help message to *hlpmsg*
    – l pathname must be relative
    – n pathname must not exist
    – o pathname must exist
    – r pathname must be readable
    – t pathname must be touchable
    – w pathname must be writable
    – W *width* format messages to *width*
               character
    – x pathname must be executable
    – y pathname must be directory
    – z pathname must be non-zero size file

HELPRANGE — Provide Help Text for Integer Range
% **/usr/sadm/bin/helprange** [*options*]
(see also **ckrange**)
Options:

- **−b** *base*   numeric base (**2-36**, **10** default)
- **−h** *hlpmsg* set help message to *hlpmsg*
- **−l** *low*   lower limit of range
- **−u** *high*   upper limit of range
- **−W** *width* format messages to *width* characters

HELPSTR — Provide Help Text for Strings
% **/usr/sadm/bin/helpstr** [*options*]
(see also **ckstr**)
Options:

- **−h** *hlpmsg* set help message to *hlpmsg*
- **−l** *len*   maximum length of input
- **−r** *regexp* match regular expression with input
  (multiple permitted; input only need match one)
- **−W** *width* format messages to *width* characters

HELPTIME — Provide Help Text for Time Value
% **/usr/sadm/bin/helptime** [*options*]
(see also **cktime**)
Options:

- **−f** *fmt*   input format:

%H	hour (00-23)
%I	hour (00-12)
%M	minute (00-59)
%p	AM or PM
%r	time as **%I:%M:%S %p**
%R	time as **%H:%M** (default)
%S	seconds (00-59)
%T	time as **%H:%M:%S**

- **−h** *hlpmsg* set help message to *hlpmsg*
- **−W** *width* format messages to *width* characters

HELPUID — Provide Help Text for User ID
% **/usr/sadm/bin/helpuid** [*options*]
(see also **ckuid**)
Options:

- **−h** *hlpmsg* set help message to *hlpmsg*
- **−m**   display list of valid logins as help
- **−W** *width* format messages to *width* characters

HELPYORN — Provide Help Text for Yes/No
% **/usr/sadm/bin/helpyorn** [*options*]
(see also **ckyorn**)
Options:

- **−h** *hlpmsg* set help message to *hlpmsg*
- **−W** *width* format messages to *width* characters

ξ **HISTORY** — Display Command Histories
% **history** [**-hr**] [*n*]
Option:
  −h   display without leading numbers
  −r   reverse order of display
n number of most recent commands to display

HOSTID — Print Host Numeric ID
% **/usr/bin/hostid**

HOSTNAME — Set/Print Host Name
% **/usr/bin/hostname**

ICONV — Code Set Converter
% **iconv −f** *from_code* **−t** *to_code* [*file*]
 stdin read if no *files* specified
Options:
  −f *from_code*
      designates input code set
  −t *to_code* designates output code set

ξ **IF** — Condition Actions on Expression Evaluations
% **if** (*condition*) *cmd*
% **if** (*condition*) **then**
 cmds
% **else if** (*condition2*) **then**
 cmds
% **else**
 cmds
% **endif**

condition a valid condition in C shell
cmd   a valid Solaris or C shell command
cmds   one or more valid Solaris or C shell
    commands

κσ **IF** — Condition Actions on Expression Evaluations
See **Control Commands** in the Solaris SHELL section
Pages 168-172

φ **INDICATOR** — Display Application Specific Alarms
  and Indicators
% **indicator** [*options*] [*strings*]
Options:
  −b *n* ring terminal bell *n* times (1-10)
  −c *col* banner start column (**0** default)
  −l *len* maximum length of display string
  −o   duplicate output to **stdout**
  −w   turn on working indicator

INDXBIB — Create Inverted Index
% **indxbib** *database*
creates entry file (**.ia** suffix) posting file (**.ib** suffix)
and tag file (**.ic** suffix) in current directory

database must reside in current directory

β INSTALL — Install Commands

% **install** [*options*] *file1 file2*
    install from *file1* to *file2*

% **install** [*options*] *files directory*
    install *files* in *directory*

% **install** **– d** [*options*] *directory*
    create *directory* (with possible parents)

Options:

– c	create directories
– d	strip executables
– g *group*	set group ID to *group* (**staff** default)
– m *mode*	set mode to *mode* (**0755** default)
– o *owner*	set owner to *owner* (super user only)
– s	strip executable files as they are copied

IPCRM — Remove Inter-Process Communications Items

% **ipcrm** [*options*]

Options:

– m *mem*	remove shared memory ID and structure
– M *mkey*	remove shared memory structure created with *mkey*
– q *msg*	remove message queue ID and structure
– Q *qkey*	remove message queue structure created with *qkey*
– s *sem*	remove semaphore ID and structure
– S *skey*	remove semaphore structure created with *skey*

IPCS — Print Inter-Process Communication Status

% **ipcs** [*options*]

Options:

– a	include all print options (**bcopt**)
– b	report info about maximum allowable sizes
– c	report creator's login and group name
– C *core*	use *core* for report (**/dev/kmem** default)
– m	report on active shared memory segments
– N *list*	report on processes in *list* (**/stand/unix** default)
– o	current message & shared memory usage
– p	report PIDs of recently active processes
– q	report on active message queues
– s	report on active semaphores
– t	report time info on recently active processes

ξ JOBS — List Information About Jobs

% **jobs** [**-l**] [%*jobid*]
    stdin read if **–** specified for *file1*

Options:

– l	report process group ID and working directory of jobs
jobid	integer identifier of job

κ **JOBS** — List Information About Jobs
% **jobs** [-p | -l] [%*jobids*]
    stdin read if − specified for *file1*
Options:

− **l**	provide more information
− **n**	show only jobs stopped/exited since last notified
− **p**	report only process ID of process group leaders of selected jobs
jobid	integer identifier of job prefaced with %

σ **JOBS** — List Information About Jobs
See **Job Control** in Solaris SHELL section
Pages 168-172

JOIN — Form the Join of Two Relations
% **join** [*options*] *file1 file2*
    stdin read if − specified for *file1*
Options:

− **1***fldnum*	Join on *fldnum*th field of file 1.
− **2***fldnum*	Join on *fldnum*th field of file 2.
− **a***n*	produce line for each unpairable line in *filen*
− **e** *str*	replace empty fields with string *str*
− **j***n m*	join on *m*th field of *filen*
− **o** *list*	specify output fields; each element of form: *n.m* where *n* is file and *m* is field, *list* is space-separated
− **t***c*	use *c* as field separator (**tab** default)
− **v***filenum*	output only unpairable line in *filenum*

σ **JSH** — Job Control Shell
% **jsh** [*options*] [*args*]
See **SH** and Solaris SHELL section
Pages 168-172

KBD — Set Keyboard State
% **kbd** [*options*]
Options:

− **c off**	turn keyclick off
− **c on**	turn keyclick on
− **d** *dev*	specify keyboard device (**/dev/kbd** default)
− **r**	reset keyboard
− **t**	return keyboard type being used

KDESTROY — Destroy Kerberos Tickets
% **/usr/bin/kdestroy** [*options*]
Options:

− **f**	do not display status message
− **n**	do not invalidate NFS credentials
− **q**	do not beep on error

KEYLOGIN — Decrypt and Store Secret Key
% **/usr/bin/keylogin**

KEYLOGOUT — Unset Secret Key on Local Machine
% **/usr/bin/keylogout**

KILL — Terminate or Send a Signal to Processes
% **/usr/bin/kill** *-s] signal pids*
% **/usr/bin/kill** **–l** [*exitstat*]
% **/usr/bin/kill** *-signal pids*
See also **Job Control Commands** in the Solaris SHELL
section Pages 168-172
Option:

– signal	decimal number of signal sent (**15** default)

common signals are:

01	hangup
02	interrupt
03	quit
09	kill (cannot be caught or ignored)
pids	process IDs to receive the signal (**0** implies all processes resulting from current login)
exitstat	exit status

KINIT — Kerberos Login Utility
% **kinit** [*options*] [*username*]
Options:

– i	prompt for Kerberos instance
– l	prompt for ticket lifetime in minutes
– r	prompt for Kerberos realm
– v	verbose

KLIST — List Current Kerberos Tickets
% **klist** [*options*]
Options:

– file *file*	use *file* as ticket file
– s	silent
– srvtab	treat *file* as service key file and print names of keys (**/etc/srvtab** if no *file* specified)
– t	check for non-expired ticket-granting-ticket only (return **0** if exists, **1** if not)

κ **KSH** — Korn Shell
% **/usr/bin/ksh** [*options*] [*args*]
% **/usr/xpg4/bin/sh** [*options*] [*args*]
% **/usr/bin/rksh** [*options*] [*args*]
Options:

– a	automatically export vars when defined
– b *cmd*	notify asynchronously of background job completions
– c *cmd*	execute *cmd*
– C	noclobber
– e	exit on error (after executing ERR trap)
– f	disable file name generation
– h	make command into tracked alias
– i	force interactive mode

(continued)

KSH, continued

– k		place variables in environment for command
– m		run background jobs as separate process group
– n		parse commands without executing them
– o *opt*		set options; can occur multiple times
	allexport	
		same as **– a**
	errexit	same as **– e**
	bgnice	lower priority of background jobs
	emacs	use emacs-style editor
	gmacs	use gmacs-style editor
	ignoreeof	
		don't exit on EOF
	keyword	
		same as **– k**
	markdirs	
		append / to generated directory names
	monitor	
		same as **– m**
	noclobber	
		prevent > from clobbering existing file
	noexec	same as **– n**
	noglob	same as **– f**
	nologi	don't save function defs in history file
	notify	same as **– b**
	nounset	
		same as **– u**
	privileged	
		same as **– p**
	trackall	
		same as **– h**
	verbose	
		same as **– v**
	vi	enter vi-style in-line editor
	viraw	process each character in vi mode
	xtrace	same as **– x**
– p		disable processing **.profile**
– r		run in restricted (**rsh**) mode
– s		sort positional parameters lexicographically
– t		exit after executing one command
– u		treat unset parameters as error
– v		echo shell input as read
– x		print commands as they are executed

KSRVTGT — Fetch Kerberos Ticket-granting Ticket
% **/usr/bin/ksrvtgt** *name instance* [*realm*] [*srvtab*]

LAST — Display Last Logins
% **last** [*options*] [*names*]
Options:

–f *file*	use *file* instead of **/var/adm/wtmpx**
–n *n*	limit output to *n* entries
–*n*	same as **-n** *n*

names   can be login names or terminals

LASTCOMM — Show Previous Commands Executed
% **lastcomm** [*command*] [*user*] [*terminal*]

command, *user* and *terminal* can be used (in any order)
to qualify the match to a particular command,
user and/or terminal ID

LD — Linkage Editor
% **/usr/ccs/bin/ld** [*options*] *files*
Options:

–a	create an absolute file (static only)
–b	make more efficient, less sharable code (dynamic only)
–B dynamic	link with **lib***x***.so first**
–B local	cause non-version definition global symbols to be reduced to local
–B reduce	cause reduction of symbolic information when generating relocatable object as per version definitions
–B static	link with **lib***x***.a**
–B symbolic[=*sym1*[,*sym2*...]]	symbolic bind of *syms* (dynamic only)
–d n	static linking
–d y	dynamic linking (default)
–D *toks*	print debug information as indicated by each *toks* to stderr
–e *symb*	set default entry point to value of *symb*
–f *name*	use symbol table as auxiliary filter on symbol table of *name*
–F *name*	use symbol table as filter on symbol table of *name*
–G	produce shared object in dynamic mode; undefined symbols allowed
–h *name*	use *name* as dynamic link name
–i	ignore **LD_LIBRARY_PATH** setting
–I *name*	specify interpreter for program header
–l *x*	search **lib***x***.so** or **lib***x***.a**
–L *dir*	add *dir* to library search list
–m	print memory map
–M *map*	use *map* as link directives
–o *output*	name of output file (**a.out** default)
–Q n	suppress tool ID information
–Q y	put tool ID information in output (default)

(continued)

LD, continued

–r		combine relocatable object files to make single file output; mutually exclusive with -a and dynamic mode
–R *path*		search list of directories specified in *path* (: separated list)
–s		strip output of symbol table and relocation bits
–t		don't warn about multiply-defined symbols
–u *symb*		enter *symb* as undefined symbol
–V		print version information
–YP,*dirlist*		use *dirlist* (delimited by :) to find libraries
–z defs		force error on undefined symbol
–z muldefs		allow multiple symbol definitions
–z nodefs		allow undefined symbols
–z noversion		don't record versioning sections
–z text		force error if relocations against non-writable allocatable section

β **LD** — Linkage Editor
% **/usr/ucb/ld** [*options*]
    works the same as non-BSD **ld** except BSD
    libraries are searched before System V libraries
Options (differences from regular **ld**):

–L *dir*		add *dir* to beginning of library search list
–Y LU,*dir*		change default *dir* used for finding libraries; deprecated and may have unexpected results

LDD — List Dynamic Dependencies
% **ldd** [*option*] *file*
Options:

–d	check all references to data objects
–f	force checking of insecure executable
–r	check all references to data objects and functions
–s	show search path used to locate shared object dependencies
–v	show all dependency relationships and requirements

κ **LET** — Evaluate Arithmetic Expressions
% **let** *args*

args evaluate each argument as arithmetic expression

LEX — Generate Lexical Analysis Programs
% **lex** [*options*] [*files*]
    stdin read if no *files* specified
Options:

–c	**C** actions (default)

(continued)

LEX, continued

– e	generate program that handles **EUC** characters; **yytext** is of type **unsigned char[]**
– n	don't print out summary
– Qn	suppress tool ID information (default)
– Qy	put tool ID information in output
– t	output to **stdout** instead of **lex.yy.c**
– v	provide summary statistics
– V	print version information
– w	generate program that handles **EUC** characters; **yytext** is of type **wchar_t[]**

ξ **LIMIT** — Set Resources Available to Shell
% **limit** [-**h**] [*resource* [*limit*]]
Options:

– h	use hard limits

LINE — Copy One Line from **stdin** to **stdout**
% **line**

LINT — C Program Checker
% **/usr/ucb/lint** [*options*] *files*
Options:

– a	suppress messages about integer assignments
– b	suppress messages about unreachable **break**s
– c	put output of second pass in **.ln** file
– C*file*	put product of first pass in *file*.**ln** file
– dirout=*dir*	
	specify directory where **.ln** files will be placed
– err=warn	
	warnings cause failure status exit just like errors
– errfmt=*fmt*	
	specify format of lint output
	fmt may be any of:

	macro	display source code, line number, error location with macro code instead of name
	simple	display line number, place number of the error in brackets
	src	display source code, line number, error location
	tab	tabular (default)

– errhdr=*h* report messages specifically for header files in comma separated list *h*, which may include any of:

	dir	check header files used which are found in directory *dir*
	no%*dir*	don't check header files used which are found in directory *dir*
	%all	all header files checked

(continued)

	%none	don't check any header files (default)
	%user	check all header files not in the /usr/include tree

– erroff=*t*   turn error messages off or on according to specifiers in comma separated list *t* of any of the following:

tag	turn off message with this *tag*
no%*tag*	turn on message with this *tag*
%all	turn off all messages
%none	turn on all messages (default)

– errtags=*a*

show the message tag for error messages (-errtags is equivalent to -errtags=yes, -errtags=no is default)

– F	print pathnames of files
– fd	reports old style function definitions or declarations
– flagsrc=*file*	
	gets lint options from *file* one option per line is the format
– h	don't apply heuristic tests
– I*dir*	search *dir* before standard ones
– k	print "lint comments"
– l*x*	include lint library **llib-l***x***.ln**
– L*dir*	search lint libraries in *dir* first
– m	suppress complaints about externals that could be static
– n	don't check compatibility against libraries
– Ncheck=*c*	

c is a comma separated list specifying checks to be made to header files:

macro	checks consistency of macros across files
extern	check for one-to-one correspondence of declarations between source files and associated header files
%all	do all -Ncheck checks
%none	do none of -Ncheck checks
no%macro	
	do none of -Ncheck macro checks
no%extern	
	do none of -Ncheck extern checks

– Nlevel=*n*   *n* is 1, 2, 3, or 4, which are as follows:

1	check done on single procedures, unconditional errors that occur on some program execution paths, but no global data nor control flow checks are done
2	(default) check whole program, global data, control flow; unconditional errors occurring in some execution paths shown

(continued)

	3	checks whole program, constant propagation, constants used as arguments, and all checks from level 2
	4	checks whole program, shows conditional errors possible under certain execution paths, and all checks from level 3

– o_lib_	create library **llib-l**_lib_**.ln**
– p	check portability with other C dialects
–R_file_	write **.ln** file to _file_ (for **cxref**)
– s	print one-line diagnostics only
– u	suppress messages about undefined or unused functions and external variables
– v	suppress messages about unused arguments
– V	print version information
– W_file_	write **.ln** file to _file_ (for **cflow**)
– x	don't report unused variables declared external
– XCC=_a_	_a_ is yes or no; when yes, C++ style comments are accepted. (-XCC is same as -XCC=yes; -XCC=no is default)
– Xexplicitpar=_a_	_a_ is yes or no; when yes, lint accepts #pragma MP directives (-Xexplicitpar is same as -Xexplicitpar=yes; -Xexplicitpar=no is default)
– Xkeeptmp=_a_	_a_ is yes or no; When yes, lint doesn't delete generated temporary files (-Xkeeptmp is same as -Xkeeptmp=yes; -Xkeeptmp=no is default)
– Xtemp=_dir_	sets directory for temporary files to _dir_; default is /tmp
– Xtime=_a_	_a_ is yes or no; when yes, lint shows execution times for each pass (-Xtime is same as -Xtime=yes; -Xtime=no is default)
– Xtransition=_a_	_a_ is yes or no; when yes, lint warns of differences between K&R C and Sun ANSI C (-Xtransition is the same as -Xtransition=yesr; -Xtransition=no is default)
– y	pretend /*LINTLIBRARY*/ directive found

Note: most **cc** command line options are recognized or ignored

β **LINT** — C Program Checker
% **/usr/ucb/lint** [_options_] _files_
Options:

– I_dir_	search _dir_ for included files

(continued)

LINT, continued
 – **L***dir*   search *dir* for library files
 – **Y P,** *dir*   Change default directory used for finding
                 libraries

LISTUSERS — List User Login Information
% **listusers** [*options*]
Options:
 – **g** *groups* list users belonging to *groups*
 – **l** *logins*   list users with specified logins

   groups and *logins* can be comma-delimited lists

LN — Make Links to Files (See **CP**)
% **/usr/bin/ln** [-**fns**] *file1* [file2]
% **/usr/xpg4/bin/ln** [-**fs**] *file1* [file2]
   make a link to *file1* named *file2*
% **/usr/bin/ln -fns**] *files directory*
% **/usr/xpg4/bin/ln** [-**fs**]] *files directory*
   make links of specified *files* in *directory*
Option:
 – **f**   force link despite target file permissions
 – **n**   don't overwrite existing file
 – **s**   create symbolic link

β **LN** — Make Links to Files
% **/usr/ucb/ln** [*options*] *file1* [*file2*]
   make a link to *file1* called *file2*
   (same name as *file1* but in current directory default)
% **/usr/ucb/ln** [*options*] *pathnames* [*directory*]
   make links of specified *files* in *directory*
Options:
 – **f**   force hard link (superuser only)
 – **s**   create symbolic links

LOADFONT — Access/Modify x86 Video Card Fonts
% **loadfont** [*option*] [*file*]
BDF here refers to Binary Distribution Format version 2.1
Options:
 – **c** *codeset*
             codeset is current font size code;
             use **?** to find out valid codesets
             available
 – **d**   write RAM font data to stdout in BDF
 – **f** *BDF_file*
             read contents of *BDF_file*
 – **m** *mode* change the console mode to *mode*
             use **?** to find out valid modes available

LOADKEYS — Load Keyboard Translation Table
% **loadkeys** [*file*]

LOCALE — display locale information
% **locale** [-**a** | -**m**]
% **locale** [**ck**] *lcategory*
Options:
 – **a**   all public locales available

(continued)

74

LOCALE, continued

– c	display names of locale categories
– k	display names and values of selected keywords
– m	display names of available charmaps
lcategory	name of a locale category

Exit Status:

0	successful
>0	error

LOCALEDEF — display locale information
% **localedef [options]** *localename*
Options:

– c	make output permanent despite any warnings
– f *charmap*	specify pathname of symbol and encoding file
– i *srcfile*	specify pathname of source definition file; **stdin** read for these if - **i** is not present
localename	identifies locale

Exit Status:

0	no errors, locale creation successful
1	warnings, but locale creation successful
2	specification exceeded implementation limits, or character set(s) not supported; locale creation failed
3	new locale creation not supported
>3	warnings or errors, no output

LOGGER — Add Entry to System Log
% **logger** [*options*] [*messages*]
Options:

– f *file*	use contents of *file* as message
– i	include **logger** PID in each line
– p *pri*	numeric or *facility*.*level* priority (**user.notice** default)
– t *tag*	mark each logged line with *tag*

Exit Status:

0	successful
>0	error

β **LOGGER** — Add Entry to System Log
% **/usr/ucb/logger** [*options*] [*messages*]
Options:

– f *file*	use contents of *file* as message
– i	include **logger** PID in each line
– p *pri*	numeric or *facility*.*level* priority (**user.notice** default)
– t *tag*	mark each logged line with *tag*

LOGIN — Sign On to System
% **login** [*option*] [*name* [*environ*]]
    login *user*, logout if no *user* specified
Options:
    −d *dir*   device to operate on
    −h *host* [*termtype*]
                 pass hostname and optionally
                 terminal type
    −p   pass environment variables
    −r *host* pass information about
                 remote *host*

LOGNAME — Print Login Name
% **logname**

ξ **LOGOUT** — Exit Login Session
% **logout**

φ **LONGLINE** — Return Length of Longest Line
% **longline** [*file*]
    if no *file* uses file from last call to **readfile**

β **LOOK** — Find Words in Dictionary or File
% **/usr/bin/look** [*options*] *string* [*file*]
Options:
    −d   dictionary order
    −f   fold case
    −t *c*   termination character *c* for *string*

/usr/share/lib/dict/words read if no *file* specified

β **LOOKBIB** — Find References in Bibliographic Database
% **lookbib** *database*

LORDER — Find Ordering Relation for Archive Files
% **lorder** *files*

LP — Send Request to Printer
% **lp** [*options*] *files*
% **lp −i** *request* [*options*]
    change options of queued request
Options:
    −c   copy rather than link files
    −d *ptr*   send request to specified printer
    −f *form* [**−d any**]
                 print on form *form*
    −H *special-handling*
               hold   suspend request
               immediate
                    print request next
               resume resume held request
    −m   send mail after printing complete
    −n *n*   print *n* copies (**1** default)

(continued)

LP, continued

- **−o** *option*   specify printer or class dependent
options as follows:
-     **cpi=***num*
  - set character pitch to *num*
  - cannot be used with **−f**
-     **length=***num*
  - set pages to *num* lines long
  - cannot be used with **−f**
-     **lpi=***num*
  - set line pitch to *num*
  - cannot be used with **−f**
-     **nobanner**
  - don't print banner page
-     **nofilebreak**
  - don't insert form feed between files
-     **stty=***num*
  - set character pitch to *num*
-     **width=***num*
  - set page width to *num* columns
  - cannot be used with **−f**
- **−p**   enable notification on completion
- **−P** *page-list*
  - print specified pages
- **−q** *pri*   assign specified priority
(**0** to **39**; **0** is highest)
- **−s**   suppress messages from **lp**
- **−S** *char-set* [**−d any**]
  - print with specified character set
  - or print-wheel
- **−t** *title*   print *title* on banner page of output
- **−T** *content_type* [**−r**]
  - print on printer that supports
  - content_type
  - **−r** indicates don't use filter
- **−w**   write to user's terminal after
printing complete
- **−y** *modes*   print according to mode list

β **LPC** — Printer Control
% **/usr/ucb/lpc** [*command* [*parameter*]]
if called with no arguments, **lpc** runs interactively

command   one from the following list
- **?** [*commands*]
  - print command help
- **abort** [**all** | [*printers*]]
  - terminate current job and disable *printer*
- **clean** [**all** | [*printers*]]
  - remove jobs from queues
- **disable** [**all** | [*printers*]]
  - turn off queues
- **down** [**all** | [*printers*]] [*message*]
  - take printer down with status message
- **enable** [**all** | [*printers*]]
  - enable queues

(continued)

LPC, continued

exit	exit from **lpc**
help [*commands*]	
	print command help
quit	exit from **lpc**
restart [**all** ǀ [*printers*]]	
	start new daemon on printer
start [**all** ǀ [*printers*]]	
	enable printing and start daemon
status [**all** ǀ [*printers*]]	
	display daemon and queue status
stop [**all** ǀ [*printers*]]	
	disable and stop after current job
topq *printer* [*jobnos*] [*users*]	
	move specified jobs (*jobnos*) or jobs
	belonging to *users* to head queue
up [**all** ǀ [*printers*]]	
	enable and start new daemon
printer	a printer name or **all** to represent
	all printers

β **LPQ** — Display Printer Queue
% **/usr/ucb/lpq** [*options*] [**+**[*interval*]] [*jobs*] [*users*]
Options:

− l	long output format
− P*ptr*	queue for printer *ptr*
	(**PRINTER** environment variable or
	default printer default)
+	continue displaying queue until empty
interval	display queue status every *interval* secs

β **LPR** — Send Request to Printer
% **/usr/ucb/lpr** *options* [*files*]
  stdin read if no *files* specified
Options:

− # *n*	print *n* copies
− c	**cifplot** data file
− C *class*	print *class* on burst page in place of
	system name
− d	**tex** data file
− f	interpret first character of each line as
	FORTRAN carriage control
− g	**plot** data file
− h	don't print burst page
− i[*n*]	indent *n* columns (**8** default)
− J *job*	print job name on burst page in place of
	file name
− l	print control chars; suppress breaks
− m	send mail after printing complete
− n	**ditroff** data file
− p	format using **pr**
− P *ptr*	send output to *ptr*
− s	print actual file, not copy or link
− t	**troff** (cat phototypesetter) data file
− T *title*	use *title* as title

(continued)

LPR, continued
    −v   raster image data file
    −w *cols* set **pr** page width to *cols*

β **LPRM** — Remove Jobs from Printer Queue
% **/usr/ucb/lprm** [*options*] [*jobnos*] [*users*]
Options:
    −   remove all jobs owned by user
    −P*ptr*   specify printer queue

jobno   number of job to remove (from **lpq**)
user   name of user owning jobs to be removed
                        (superuser only)

LPSTAT — Print Status of Printer System
% **lpstat** [*options*]
Options:
    −a [*list1*] print acceptance status of destinations
    −c [*classnames*]
                  print *classnames* and members
    −d   print default destination for **lp**
    −f [*forms*] [**−l**]
                  verify that specified forms are recognized
                  (**all** default)
                  −l lists form descriptions
    −o [*list2*] print status of printer requests
    −p [*ptrs*] [**−D**] [**−l**]
                  print status of specified printers
                  −D print printer description list
                  −l print full description for local printers
    −P   print paper types
    −r   print information on the **lp** request
                  scheduler
    −R   show position of job in queue
    −s   print summary system statistics
    −S [*csets*] [**−l**]
                  verify that specified character sets are
                  recognized (**all** default)
                  −l append list of devices
    −t   print all status information
    −u [*users*] print information on *user*'s requests
    −v [*ptrs*] print list of pathnames for printers
    list1   list of printer and class names
    list2   list of printer names, class names,
                  request IDs
    users   may include system name (**all** means all)

β **LPTEST** — Generate Lineprinter Ripple Pattern
% **/usr/ucb/lptest** [*length* [*count*]]

length   output line length
count   number of output lines

LS — List Contents of Directories

% **/usr/bin/ls** [*options*] [*filespecs*]

% **/usr/xpg4/bin/ls** [*options*] [*filespecs*]
    current working directory used if no *directories*
    specified

Options:

–1	print one entry per line
–a	list all entries (including ones starting with .)
–A	as **–a** but . and .. not listed
–b	print non-printing characters as octal
–c	use time file created or mode changed in **–t** & **–l** options
–C	multi-column output with entries sorted down
–d	list only name (not contents) of directory
–f	interpret each argument as directory
–F	print / after directories, * after executables, @ after symbolic links
–g	like **–l** but don't print owner
–i	print inode number
–l	long list (mode, links, owner, group, size, modification time)
–L	list file referenced by link (instead of link itself)
–m	print files across, separated by commas
–n	like **–l** but use numeric user and group ID
–o	like **–l** but don't print group
–p	mark directories with /
–q	print non-printing characters as a **?**
–r	reverse sort order
–R	recursively list subdirectories
–s	print size in blocks
–t	sort by modification time
–u	use time of last access in **–t** & **–l** options
–x	multi-column list, sorted across each row

β **LS** — List Contents of Directories

% **/usr/ucb/ls** [*options*] [*paths*]
    current working directory used if no *directories*
    specified

Options:

–1	force one entry per line format
–a	list all entries (includes ones starting with .)
–A	as **–a** but . and .. not listed
–c	use time of last change for sort and print
–C	force multi-column output
–d	list only directory, not contents
–f	force *files* to be treated as directories
–F	print / after directories; * after executables, @ after symbolic links, = after sockets
–g	show group ownership in long output
–i	print inode number

(continued)

LS, continued

−l	long list (mode, links, owner, size, modifcation time)
−L	list file referenced by link
−q	display non-printing characters as ?
−r	reverse sort order
−R	recursively list subdirectories
−s	print size in kilobytes
−t	sort by modification time
−u	use time of last access in **−t** & **−l**

paths can be directory or file names

M4 — Macro Preprocessor
% **/usr/ccs/bin/m4** [*options*] [*files*]
% **/usr/xpg4/bin/m4** [*options*] [*files*]
    stdin read if − or no *files* specified
Options:

−B*n*	size of push-back & arg buffers (**4096** default)
−D*name* [**=***val*]	
	define *name* to *val* (**null** default)
−e	operate interactively
−H*n*	hash array size *n* (**199** default)
−s	enable line sync output for C preprocessor
−S*n*	call stack size (**100** default)
−T*n*	token buffer size (**512** default)
−U*name*	undefine *name*

MACH — Display Processor Type
% **/usr/bin/mach**

MAIL — Send or Read Mail
% **mail** [*options*] *users*
    send message from **stdin** to *users*
Send Mail Options:

−m *mtype*	add **Message-Type:** *mtype*
−t	include list of people **mail** sent to in **To:** lines
−w	don't wait for completion of remote transfer program to send to remote user

% **mail** [*options*]
Read Mail Options:

−e	don't print mail, return exit value **0** if mail, **1** if no mail
−f*file*	use *file* instead of **/var/mail/***user*
−h	print headers only, then **?** prompt
−p	print all messages, no prompt for disposition
−P	print all messages, all header lines
−q	terminate after interrupt
−r	print messages in first-in, first-out order

Debug Mail Options:

− x *n*   create trace file (**/tmp/MLDBG***pid*)
with debug information at debug level *n*
retained on error if *n*>0;
always retained if *n*<0

Exit Status:

0	successful when user had mail
1	user had no mail or initialization error
>1	error

β **MAIL** — Send or Read Mail (see also **mail**)
% **/usr/ucb/mail** [*options*] [*users*]
% **/usr/ucb/Mail** [*options*] [*users*]
     Arguments same as for **mailx**

β **MAILCOMPAT** — Set SunOS Compatibility for Solaris Mailbox
% **mailcompat**

β **MAILSTATS** — Display Sendmail Statistics
% **mailstats** [*options*] [*statfile*]

options:

− c *configfile*
          specify sendmail configuration file
− f *statisticsfile*
          specify sendmail statistics file

MAILX — Send or Read Mail (see also **mail**)
Options (These 5 work with either Send or Read Mail):

− b*bcc*   set blind carbon copy list to *bcc*;
bcc must be in quotes if more than one name
− B   don't buffer input and output
− c*cc*   set carbon copy list to *bcc*;
cc must be in quotes if more than one name
− d   show debug output
− i   ignore interrupts
− n   disable reading of **/etc/mail/mailx.rc**
− V   print version information

% **mailx** [*options*] *users*
     send message from **stdin** to *users*
Send Mail Options:

− F   record output in file named *user1*
− h *n*   *n* network hops made so far
− r *address* pass *address* as return address
to delivery program
− s *subject* set subject heading to *subject*
− U   convert **uucp** address to internet format
− v   pass **− v** flag to **sendmail**
− ˜   enable ˜ escape sequences
(default if input is **stdin**

(continued)

MAILX, continued
% **mailx** [*options*]
Read Mail Options:

– e	check for mail, return **0** if mail is present
– f [*file*]	read messages from *file*, (**mbox** default)
– f [**+***folder*]	
	use the file *folder* in the folder directory
– H	only print header summary
– I	include group and ID header lines in output
– N	don't print header summary
– t	read **cc** and **bcc** headers to determine recipient
– T *file*	record headers in *file*
– u *user*	read *user*'s mail

MAKE — Maintain Program Groups
% **/usr/ccs/bin/make** [*options*] [*names*]
Options:

– d	give reasons why **make** rebuilds target; display newer dependencies
– dd	show dependency check and processing in detail
– D	display text of makefiles that were read in
– DD	display text of makefiles, **make.rules** file, state file, and hidden-dependency reports
– e	environment variables override **makefile**
– f *makefile*	
	specify name of description file (**makefile**, **Makefile**, **s.makefile**, **s.Makefile** defaults) *makefile* named **–** uses **stdin**
– i	ignore errors of invoked commands
– k	abort current entry on error; continue with unrelated entries
– K*state*	the specified *state* file
– n	print but don't execute commands
– p	print macro definitions and target descriptions
– P	merely report dependencies, don't build them
– q	successful exit status if target file is current
– r	do not use built-in rules in file **/usr/share/lib/make/make.rules**
– s	do not print commands before executing
– S	undo effect of **– k** option; stop processing when non-zero exit status returned
– t	update target files by **touch**ing them
– V	set SysV mode

MAN — Display Reference Manual Pages
% **man** [*options*] [**– s** *section*] *titles*
% **man** [**– M**] **– k** *keywords*
% **man** [**– M**] **– f** *files*
Options:

–	don't send output through **pg** (**more**)
– a	show all man pages matching *title*
– d	debug
– f *files*	locate manual pages related to *files*
– F	force search of all directories
– k *keyword*	
	search for keyword in summaries of **windex** database
– l	list all man pages found matching *title*
– M *path*	use *path* as : separated search list for man files
– r	reformat, don't display man page
– s *sec*	search *section*
– t	**troff** output (first form only)
– T *mac*	use *mac* macro package (**man** default)

MCONNECT — Connect to SMTP Mail Server
% **mconnect** [*options*] [*hostname*]
Options:

– p *port*	specify SMTP port (**25** default)
– r	raw mode

MCS — Manipulate Comment Section of Object File
% **mcs** [*options*] *file*
Options:

– a *string*	append *string* to comment section
– c	compress comment section
– d	delete comment section
– n *section*	access *section* (**.comment** default)
– p	print comment section
– V	print version information on **stderr**

MESG — Permit or Deny Messages via **write** or **talk**
% **mesg** [*option*] [**n** | **y**]
current message state printed if no *option* specified
Options:

–n	deny messages
n	deny messages
–y	allow messages
y	allow messages

Exit Status:

0	messages receivable
1	messages not receivable
2	error

ϕ **MESSAGE** — Put Arguments on Message Line
% **message** [*options*] [*string*]
stdin read if no *string*
Options:

– b [*n*]	ring bell *n* times (**1** default)
– f	set message duration to "frame"

(continued)

84

MESSAGE, continued

	– o	duplicate message on **stdout**
	– p	set message duration to "permanent"
	– t	set message duration to "transient"
	– w	turn on working indicator
string		message to put on FMLI message line

MKDIR — Create Specified Directories
% **mkdir** [*options*] *dirnames*
Options:
    – m *mode* specify directory's mode (see **chmod**)
    – p   create parent directories that don't exist

MKMSGS — Create Message Files from Strings
% **mkmsgs** [*options*] *stringfile msgfile*
Options:
    – i *locale* put *msgfile* in directory
                 /usr/lib/locale/*locale***/LC_MESSAGES**
    – o   overwrite *msgfile*

β **MKSTR** — Create Error Message File
% **/usr/ucb/mkmsgs** [-] *msgfile prefix file*
Options:
    –   place message at end of specified
              message file

msgfile	message file
prefix	output file prefix
file	output file

MORE — View File by Screenful or by Line
% **/usr/bin/more** [**-cdflrsuw**] [*-lines*] [+*lineno*]
    [+/*pattern*] [*files*]
% **/usr/xpg4/bin/more** [**-cdeisu**] [**-n***n*] [**-p***cmd*]
    [**-t***tagstr*] [*files*]
% **/usr/xpg4/bin/more** [**-cdeisu**] [**-n***n*] [+*cmd*]
    [**-t***tagstr*] [*files*]
Options:
    +*/pat*   start 2 lines before line containing **pat**
    – c   redraw instead of scroll
    – d   display error message on invalid
              command
    – e   exit immediately after last line
    – f   count by <newlines> instead of
              screen lines
    – i   pattern matching case independent
    – l   treat formfeed (^**L**) as ordinary character
    – n*n*   (*n*) lines per screenful
    – p*cmd* execute **more** internal command (*cmd*)
              for each file
    – *n*   window size (default set with **stty**)
    + *n*   start viewing file at line *n*
    – r   display control characters as ^*c*
    – s   reduce multiple blank lines to one
    – t*tagstr* write screenful of file
              containing *tagstr*

(continued)

MORE, continued

– u	suppress terminal underlining or enhancing (/usr/bin version)
– u	print backspace as ˆ**H** (/usr/xpg4/bin version)
– w	prompt before exiting (any key terminates)

MSGFMT — Create Message Object
% **msgfmt** [*options*] *file***.po**
Options:

– o	*outfile*	put output in *outfile*
– v		verbose

MT — Magnetic Tape Control
% **mt** [*option*] *command* [*count*]
Option:

– f [*device*]	name of tape device (value of TAPE environment variable or **/dev/rmt12** default)

command	tape command to perform
asf	absolute forward to file *count*
bsf	backspace *count* marks
bsr	backspace *count* records
eof	write *count* eof marks
eom	space to end of recorded media (SCSI only)
erase	erase entire tape
fsf	forward space *count* files
fsr	forward space *count* records
nbsf	position to first block of back *count* files
offline	rewind, unload, take drive offline
retension	retension the tape
rewind	rewind
rewoffl	rewind, unload, take drive offline
status	print tape unit status
weof	write *count* eof marks
count	repeat count for *command* (**1** default)

MV — Move Files (See **CP**)
% **/usr/bin/mv** [*options*] *file1 file2*
    rename (or move) *file1* to *file2*
% **/usr/bin/mv** [*options*] *files directory*
    rename (or move) specified *files* to *directory*
% **/usr/xpg4/bin/mv** [*options*] *file1 file2*
    rename (or move) *file1* to *file2*
% **/usr/xpg4/bin/mv** [*options*] *files directory*
    rename (or move) specified *files* to *directory*
Options:

– f	force move despite target file permissions
– i	ask for confirmation before overwriting target

NAWK — Pattern Scanning Language
    (See Pages 163-167)
% **/usr/bin/nawk** [*options*] [*prog*] [*files*]
% **/usr/xpg4/bin/awk** [*options*] [*prog*] [*files*]
    stdin read if – or no *files* specified
Options:
– f	*pfile*	use *pfile* as program
– Fc		field separator character is c
– v	*var=val*	
		assign *val* to nawk variable *var*
prog		program line (should be in single quotes)

NEQN — Typeset Mathematics
% **neqn** *files*
    stdin read if no *files* specified

NEWALIASES — Rebuild Mail Aliases Database
% **newaliases**

NEWFORM — Change Text File Format
% **newform** [**– s**] [*options*] [*files*]
    stdin read if no *files* specified
Options:
– an	append n characters to end of line
– bn	truncate n characters from beginning of line
– ck	set prefix/suffix character to k (space default)
– en	truncate n characters from end of line
– f	write tab format before output (**– 8** default)
– i$format$	set tab format (**– 8** default)
– ln	set line length to n characters (**72** default)
– o$format$	replace spaces by tabs according to tab format (**– 8** default)
– pn	prefix n characters to beginning of line
– s	remove characters before first tab, place up to 8 at the end of the line

NEWGRP — Log In to a New Group
% **/usr/bin/newgrp** [*options*] [*group*]
Options:
-l	adopt new group's environment
-	adopt new group's environment

NEWS — Print News Items
% **news** [*options*] [*items*]
Options:
– a	print all items
– n	print names, not content of current items
– s	print number of current items

NICE — Run Command at Low Priority
% **/usr/bin/nice** [*option*] *command* [*args*]
    priority lowered by 10 if *option* not specified
Option:
    − *n*   lower scheduling priority by *n*, range 1–19

ξ **NICE** — Run Command at Low Priority
% **nice** [+ *n*] [*cmd*]
% **nice** [- *n*] [*cmd*]
    priority lowered by 10 if *option* not specified

n   scheduling priority increment
cmd   command to run in C shell at lowered
                 priority

NIS+ — Network Information Name Service
(See specific NIS commands below)

Definitions:
    credential – a piece of information that allows one
    to be identified. This applies to both users and
    hosts. If a secure communication channel is used,
    then the information is considered to be
    "secure credentials".

    domain – a grouping of maps (namespace) that
    is governed by a single authority.

    object – the basic unit in a namespace. It has two
    parts–the actual data and the system/administrative
    part (e.g. access rights).

    principal – a user or host that requests service and
    has valid credentials.

NISCAT — Display NIS+ Tables and Objects
% **niscat** [*options*] *tables*
% **niscat** [*options*] − **o** *names*
Options:
    − **A**   display table data and data in tables
                       in initial table's concatenation path
    − **h**   display header line before table
    − **L**   follow links
    − **M**   send request to master server only
    − **o** *name*   display internal representation
                       of NIS+ object *name*
    − **P**   follow concatenation path (with − **o**)
    − **v**   display binary data (***B*** default)

NISCHGRP — Change Group of NIS+ Object
% **nischgrp** [*options*] *group names*
Options:
    − **A**   modify all entries; implies − **P**
    − **f**   force operation; fail silently
    − **L**   follow links; change owner of linked
                       object, not of link
    − **P**   follow concatenation path

(continued)

NISCHGRP, continued

name   NIS+ object or entry

NISCHMOD — Change Access Permissions of Object
% **nischmod** [*options*] *mode names*
Options:
– A	modify all entries; implies **– P**
– f	force operation; fail silently
– L	follow links; change owner of linked object, not of link
– P	follow concatenation path

mode   comma-delimited list of *rights* of the form:
     [*who*] *op perm* [*op perm*] ...
    who is a combination of
	a	all (same as **owg**)
	g	group
	n	nobody (unauthenticated clients)
	o	owner
	w	world

  op is one of
	+	add permission
	–	remove permission
	=	set permissions equal to *perm*

 perm is a combination of
	c	create
	d	destroy
	m	modify
	r	read

NISCHOWN — Change Owner of NIS+ Object
% **nischown** [*options*] *owner names*
Options:
– A	modify all entries; implies **– P**
– f	force operation; fail silently
– L	follow links; change owner of linked object, not of link
– P	follow concatenation path

NISCHTTL — Change Time to Live of NIS+ Object
% **nischttl** [*options*] *time names*
Options:
– A	modify all entries; implies **– P**
– f	force operation; fail silently
– L	follow links; change owner of linked object, not of link
– P	follow concatenation path

time   time to live in seconds or combination of
*n***d**	*n* days
*n***h**	*n* hours
*n***m**	*n* minutes
*n***s**	*n* seconds

NISDEFAULTS — Display NIS+ Defaults
% **nisdefaults** [*options*]
Options:
– a	all defaults in terse format

(continued)

NISDEFAULTS, continued

– **d**	default domain name
– **g**	default group name
– **h**	default host name
– **p**	default principal name
– **r**	default access rights
– **s**	default directory search path
– **t**	default time to live
– **v**	verbose format

NISERROR — Display NIS+ Error Message
% **niserror** *error_num*

NISGREP — Search NIS+ Tables
% **nisgrep** [*options*] *keypats table*
Options:

– **A**	return all data
– **c**	display count of matches only
– **h**	display headers for tables
– **M**	get information from master server only
– **o**	display internal representation of matching objects
– **P**	follow concatenation path
– **v**	verbose; don't suppress display of binary data
keypats	either a regular expression to match a key in the first column or any number of matches of the form
col=re	where:
	col name of column to search
	re regular expression to match in column
table	name of NIS+ table to search

NISGRPADM — NIS+ Group Administration
% **nisgrpadm** [*options*] *group principals*
Options:

– **a**	add NIS+ principals to *group*
– **c**	create *group* in NIS+ namespace
– **d**	destroy group in NIS+ namespace
– **l**	list effective membership in group
– **M**	master server only
– **r**	remove *principals* from *group*
– **s**	silent; return results in exit status
– **t**	test *principals* specified for membership in *group*

NISLN — Symbolically Link NIS+ Objects
% **nisln** [*options*] *name linkname*
Options:
   – **D** *defaults*

> set defaults from colon-separated list:
> **access=***rights*
>> access permissions
>> (----**rmcdr**--**r**--- default)
> **group=***groupname*

(continued)

NISLN, continued

        owner=_ownername_
        ttl=_time_ time to live (**12 hours** default)
  – L   follow links; change owner of linked
        object, not of link

NISLS — List Contents of NIS+ Directory
% **nisls** [_options_] [_names_]
Options:

– d	treat directories like other objects; don't list contents
– g	display group rather than owner
– l	long format output
– L	follow links
– m	display modification rather than creation time
– M	get information from master server
– R	recursively list subdirectories

NISMATCH — Search NIS+ Tables
% **nismatch** [_options_] _keyspecs table_
% **nismatch** [_options_] _indexedname_
Options:

– A	return all data
– c	display count of matches only
– h	display headers for tables
– M	get information from master server only
– o	display internal representation of matching objects
– P	follow concatenation path
– v	verbose; don't suppress display of binary data

indexedname	search criteria plus table name in format: [_col=value_]**,**_table.directory_
keyspecs	either a key to search for in the first column or any number of matches of the form:
col=value	where:
col	name of column to search
value	value to match in column
table	name of NIS+ table to search

NISMKDIR — Create NIS+ Directories
% **nismkdir** [_options_] _dirname_
Options:

  – D _defaults_

        set defaults from colon-separated list:
        access=_rights_
            access permissions
            (----**rmcdr--r---** default)
        group=_groupname_
        owner=_ownername_
        ttl=_time_ time to live (**12 hours** default)

(continued)

NISMKDIR, continued

−m *hostname*

> if *dirname* does not exist, create it with *hostname* as master server; otherwise, change master server to *hostname*

−s *hostname*

> replicate *dirname* on host *hostname*

NISPASSWD — Change NIS+ Password Information

% **nispasswd** [*options*] [*username*]

> change password information

Options:

−a   show all entries

−d [*userid*]

> display information for *userid*

−D *domain*

> consult **password.org_dir** table on *domain*

−f   expire password (forcing change at next login)

−g   change gecos (finger) field information

−h   change home directory

−l   lock password entry

−s   change login shell

−n *days*   set minimum days for password to *days*

−w *days*   warn user *days* before password expires

−x *days*   set maximum days for password to *days*

Exit Status:

0	success
1	permission denied
2	invalid option combination
3	unexpected failure; table not changed
4	NIS+ passwd table missing
5	NIS+ busy
6	invalid argument to option
7	password aging disabled

NISRM — Remove Objects from NIS+ Namespace

% **nisrm** [*options*] [*names*]

Options:

−f   force removal

−i   ask for confirmation before each delete

NISRMDIR — Remove NIS+ Directories

% **nisrmdir** [*options*] [*dirnames*]

Options:

−f   force removal

−i   ask for confirmation before each delete

−s *hostname*

> remove host *hostname* as replica for *dirname* only (master server and all replicas removed by default)

NISTBLADM — Administer NIS+ Tables
% **nistbladm** *func* [*options*] [*names*]
    create, add to, update, remove from table
% **nistbladm** **−d** *table*
    delete empty table

Options:

−D *defaults*	
	specify defaults with **−a** or **−c**
−p *path*	search path (colon-separated list)
−s *sep*	separator character (space default)
−t *type*	table type (**−u** only)

Functions:

func	function to perform
−a	add new table entry
−A	add new table entry or overwrite old
−c	create new table
−m	modify table entry
−r	remove one table entry
−R	remove matching table entries
−u	update table attributes (concatenation path, separation character, column access rights and type)

names	either *indexednames* or *col=value* list and *tablename*

NISTEST — Conditional Test in NIS+ Namespace
% **nistest** [*options*] [*name*]

Options:

−a *rights*	test if process has specified access rights (see **nischmod**)	
−A	all data (for indexed names or links)	
−L	follow links	
−M	get information from master server	
−P	follow concatenation path	
−t *type*	test type of object	
	D	directory
	G	group
	L	link
	P	private
	T	table

name	either an object or an indexed name

Exit Status:

0	success
1	not a match
2	illegal usage

NL — Line Numbering Filter
% **/usr/bin/nl** [*options*] [*file*]
% **/usr/xpg4/bin/nl** [*options*] [*file*]
    stdin read if no *file* specified
Options:

– b*type*	number specified lines:	
	Types:	
	a	all lines
	n	no lines
	p*re*	lines containing regular expression *re*
	t	lines with text only (default)
– d*xx*	specify delimiters for start of logical page section (\: default)	
– f*type*	like **– b** except for footer (**n** default)	
– h*type*	like **– b** except for header (**n** default)	
– i*n*	page number increment (**1** default)	
– l*n*	*n* blank lines treated as one (**1** default)	
– n*format*	line numbering format:	
	ln left justify, zero suppressed	
	rn right justify, zero suppressed (default)	
	rz right justify, zero filled	
– p	don't restart numbers at logical page end	
– s*c*	use *c* between number and text (**tab** default)	
– v*n*	number first page *n* (**1** default)	
– w*n*	set size of number field (**6** default)	

NM — Print Symbol Table
% **/usr/ccs/bin/nm** [*options*] *files*
% **/usr/xpg4/bin/nm** [*options*] *files*
Options:

– A	print full path or library name
– C	print C++ names decoded
– g	print only global symbol information
– h	don't print header
– l	flag "weak" symbols with an *****
– n	sort external symbols by name
– o	print value & size in octal (decimal default)
– p	produce parsed output
– P	output portable and to **stdout**
– r	print name of archive or object file before each line
– R	print archive name, object file and symbol name
– s	print section name instead of section index
– t d	print number in decimal format
– t o	print number in octal format
– t x	print number in hexidecimal format
– u	print undefined symbols only
– v	sort external symbols by value
– V	print version information
– x	print value & size in hexadecimal

NOHUP — Run Command Ignoring Hangups
% **/usr/bin/nohup** command [args]
% **/usr/xpg4/bin/nohup** command [args]

ξ **NOTIFY** — Notify Asynchronously of Job Status
    Changes
% **notify** [%jobids]

NROFF — Text Formatter
% **nroff** [options] [files]
    stdin read if no files specified
Options:

– e	equally spaced words in justified lines
– h	speed output with tabs
	(set every 8 spaces)
– i	read **stdin** after all files
– mname	prepend macro file
	/usr/share/lib/tmac/tmac.name
– nn	number first page n
– olist	print only listed page numbers
– q	invoke simultaneous input/output mode
	of **.rd**
– ran	set number register a to n
	(a is one character only)
– s[n]	stop every n pages (**1** default)
– Tname	specify output device type
– un	set emboldening for font on
	position 3 to n
list	comma-separated, n–m is range, –n
	is beginning to page n, n– is page n to end

OD — File Dump
% **/usr/bin/od** [options] [file] [[**+**]offset[base][**b**]]
% **/usr/xpg4/bin/od** [options] [file] [[**+**]offset[base][**b**]]
    stdin read if no file specified
Options:

– Aoffset_base	
	specify input offset base
– b	byte dump in octal
– c	byte dump in ASCII characters, except
	some non-graphic characters as C-escape
	codes (same as **-C** with xpg4 version)
– C	interpret bytes according to **LC-CTYPE**
	setting; some non-graphic characters as
	C-escape codes
– d	word dump in unsigned decimal
– D	long word dump in unsigned decimal
– f	long word dump in floating point
– F	double long word dump in floating point
– js	skip s bytes from beginning
	of input
– Ncnt	format no more than cnt bytes of input
– o	word dump in octal (default)
– O	long word dump in octal
– s	word dump in signed decimal

(continued)

OD, continued

– S		long word dump in signed decimal
– S		long word dump in signed decimal
– t*typestr*		Specify output types by the following codes:
	a	interpret bytes as named characters
	c	interpret bytes according to **LC-CTYPE** locale category (may be multi-byte characters)
	d*n*	decimal integer of *n* bytes
		C also used for 1 byte integer
		S also used for 2 byte integer
		I also used for 4 byte integer
		L also used for 8 byte integer
	f*n*	floating point of *n* bytes
		F also used for 2 byte float
		D also used for 4 byte float
		L also used for 8 byte float
	o*n*	octal integer of *n* bytes
		C, **S**, **I**, or **L** may also be used as with decimal integer indicator
	u*n*	unsigned integer of *n* bytes
		C, **S**, **I**, or **L** may also be used as with decimal integer indicator
	x*n*	hexidecimal integer of *n* bytes
		C, **S**, **I**, or **L** may also be used as with decimal integer indicator
– v		verbose output
– x		word dump in hexadecimal
– X		long word dump in hexadecimal
offset		specify octal offset to start dumping *file*
+		required if *file* is omitted
base		base for offset and addresses (octal default)
	.	decimal
	x	hexadecimal
b		indicate offset is in 512 byte blocks
B		indicate offset is in 512 byte blocks

ON — Execute Command on Remote System
% **on** [*options*] *host command* [*args*]
Options:

– d	debug mode
– i	interactive mode
– n	no input (return EOF on read from **stdin**)

ξ **ONINTR** — C Shell Interrupt Control
% **onintr** [- | *label*]
   If no options specified, restore default shell action on interrupts.
Options:

–	ignore all interrupts
label	execute goto label on interrupt

PACK — Compress Files
% **pack** [*options*] *files*
files are compressed to *files***.z**; originals removed
Options:
–	print statistical information on **stdout**
–f	force packing of *files*

PAGE — View File by Screenful or by Line (See **MORE**)
% **page** [*options*] *files*

PAGESIZE — Display Size of Memory Page
% **/usr/bin/pagesize**

β **PAGESIZE** — Display Size of Memory Page
% **pagesize**

PASSWD — Change Login Password
% **passwd** [*options*] [*name*]
Option:
–d		delete password for *name*
–D *domain*		
		consult passwd.org_dir table in *domain*
–e		change the login shell
–f		expire password and force user
		to change it next login
–g		change gecos (finger) information
–h		change home directory
–l		lock password entry for *name*
–n *min*		set minimum days for password
–r *rep*		specifies password repository *rep*
		rep may be: **files**, **nis**, or **nisplus**
–s *name*		display password attributes for *name*
–w *warn*		set *warn* field for *name*
–x *max*		set maximum days for password

[*name*] is the user's login name

Exit Status:
0	successful
1	permission denied
2	invalid option combination
3	password file(s) unchanged
4	password file(s) missing
5	password file(s) busy
6	invalid option argument

PASTE — Horizontally Concatenate Files
% **paste** [*options*] *files*
    stdin read if **–** specified in *files*
Options:
–d*list*	use *list* chars as line separators
	(**tab** default)
–s	merge subsequent lines from one file
list	characters reused when exhausted

PATCH — Apply Changes to Files
% **patch** [*options*] *file*
Options:

–b	save copy contents of original files
–c	see patch file as context difference (like output of **diff** -c)
–d*dir*	change current directory to *dir* before processing
–D*def*	mark changes using C preprocessor construct with existence of *def* as a condition
–e	interpret patch file as **ed** script instead of *diff* script
–i*pfile*	read *pfile* for patch instead of **stdin**
–l	cause unequal spaces to match
–n	interpret script as normal difference
–N	ignore already applied patches (default)
–o*outfile*	write copy of file referenced by each patch to*outfile*
–p*n*	delete *n* patch name components from the start of each path name
–r*rfile*	specify reject file *rfile*
–R	reverse sense of patch script
file	A path name of a file to patch

PATHCHK — Check Path Names
% **pathchk** [*option*] [*path*]
Options:

–p	check syntax relative to **_POSIX_PATH_MAX**, checking for characters not in portable filename set, and ignoring underlying filesystem

φ **PATHCONV** — Convert Alias to Its Pathname
% **pathconv** [*options*] [*files*]
    stdin read if no **–v** option
Options:

–f	return full pathname (default)
–l	use < and > at trimmed ends
–n*n*	trim to *n* characters max (1 to 255)
–t	trim pathname to displayable form
–v *arg*	specify alias using **fmli** alias file (*alias_file*) if used with **–t** option, *arg* is a string rather than alias reference

PAX — Portable Archive Interchange
% **pax** [*options*] [*pattern*]
% **pax** [*options*] [*file*]
% **pax** [*options*] [*file*] *dir*
Options:

–a	append files to end of archive
–b*b*	set blocksize of output by decimal *b*

(continued)

– c	match all but the specified files or archive members
– d	don't match directory trees rooted at specified files
– f*arf*	specify path name *arf* of archive
– i	interactively rename files or archive members
– k	prevent overwriting existing files
– l	link files
– n	get first archive member that matches each *pattern* operand
– o*opts*	reserved for format specific options
– p*str*	specify characteristics options

	a	don't preserve file access times
	e	preserve user and group ID, file mode bits, access and modification times
	m	don't preserve file modification times
	o	preserve user and group ID
	p	preserve file mode bits

– r	read archive file from **stdin**
– s*rstr*	use substitution expression *rstr* to modify *pattern* or *file* operands
– t	preserve access times from before **pax** read
– u	ignore older files
– v	verbose table of contents in list mode (**stdout**) or write archive member patch names to **stderr**
– w*fmt*	write to **stdout**
– x*fmt*	specify output archive format *fmt* as **cpio** or **ustar**
– X	don't cross device ID partitions when going through directory trees

PCAT — Unpack and Concatenate Packed Files
(See **PACK**)
% **pcat** *files*
  unpacked files written to **stdout**

PCMAPKEYS — Set Keyboard Extended Map and
  Scancode Translation
% **pcmapkeys** [*options*]
Options:

– d	temporarily disable compose key and deadkey sequences under extended mapping
– e	enables compose key and deadkey sequences under extended mapping
– f*map*	install contents of *map* file
– g	display current mappings
– n	disable/dismantle extended mapping

π PCRED — Display Credentials of Processes
% **/usr/proc/bin/pcred** *pids*

pids   process IDs

π PFILES — Display File Info for Processes
% **/usr/proc/bin/pfiles** *pids*

pids   process IDs

π PFLAGS — Display /proc Status Info
% **/usr/proc/bin/pflags** *pids*

pids   process IDs

PG — View File by Screenful
% **pg** [*options*] [*files*]
Options:
+ /*pattern***/**	start at first line containing *pattern*
+ *n*	start at line *n*
− *n*	window is *n* lines
− c	clear screen for each page
− e	don't pause at end of file
− f	don't split long lines
− n	don't need newline after command letters
− p *prompt*	set prompt to *prompt*, (**:** default)
	%d specifies page number
− r	restricted mode – disable shell escape
− s	print messages and prompts in reverse video

enter **h** to display a list of commands

PKGINFO — Display Software Package Info
% **pkginfo** [*options*] [*pkgs*]
    stdin read if no **−v** option
Options:
− a *arch*	specify package architecture
− c *catlist*	comma-delimited list of categories to match package
− d *dev*	pathname where package resides; use **spool** to indicate default installation spool directory
− i	info on fully installed packages only
− l	long format listing
− p	info on partially installed packages only
− q	no listing; status check only
− r	list installation base of relocatables
− R *rpath*	set root directory to be subdirectory path name of *rpath*
− v *ver*	version of package to list (use ˜*ver* for all compatible with *ver*)
− x	extracted listing
pkg	package abbreviation or instance (use *pkg*.* for all instances)

PKGMK — Produce Installable Package
% **pkgmk** [*options*] [*pkgs*]
Options:

−a *arch*	override architecture info from **pkginfo** file
−b *basedir*	prepend *basedir* to source location
−d *dev*	create package on *dev* (installation spool directory default)
−f *proto*	use *proto* as input to command (**Prototype** or **prototype** default)
−l *limit*	maximum size in blocks of output device
−o	overwrite existing package if same instance
−p *pstamp*	override production stamp definition
−r *rootpath*	override destination paths in **prototype** file with *rootpath*
−v *ver*	override version info with *ver*
var=value	place variable definition in package environment
pkg	package abbreviation or instance (use *pkg.** for all instances)

PKGPARAM — Display Package Parameter Values
% **pkgparam** [*options*] [*params*]
Options:

−d *dev*	pathname where package resides; use **spool** to indicate default installation spool directory
−f *file*	read parameters from *file*
pkginst	package instance (required unless **−f** used)
−R *root_path*	define full pathname of root directory
−v	verbose mode; show parameter names and values
param	parameter whose value should be displayed (all parameters default)

PKGPROTO — Generate Prototype File
% **pkgproto** [*options*] [*pathstrs*]
    paths read from **stdin** if no *pathstrs*
Options:

−c *class*	map class of paths to *class*
−i	ignore symbolic links (record paths as **ftype=f**, not **ftype=s**)

pathstr can be of either of the following forms:

path	path of directory where objects located
path=subpath	locate object in *path* but substitute *subpath* into output

PKGTRANS — Translate Package Format
% **pkgtrans** [*options*] *dev1 dev2 pkginsts*
    paths read from **stdin** read if *path* options
Options:

– i	copy **pkginfo** and **pkgmap** files only
– n	create new instance of package if any exists
– o	overwrite existing package instance
– s	write to *dev2* as datastream instead of filesystem

dev1	source device
dev2	destination device
pkginst	package name with optional *.instance*

π **PLDD** — Display Dynamic Libraries of Processes
% **/usr/proc/bin/pldd** *pids*

pids	process ids

PLOT — Graphics Filter(s) for Plotters
% **/usr/ucb/plot** [-**T** *terminal*]
(The commands **aedplot, bgplot, crtplot, dumbplot, gigiplot, hpplot, implot, plottoa, t300, t300s, t4013, t450, tek, vplot, hp7221plot** all have the above syntax and will not otherwise be mentioned in this reference)
terminal may be any of the following:

2648 or **2648a** or **h8** or **hp2648** or **hp2648a**	
	HP 2648
hp7221 or **hp7** or **h7**	
	HP 7221
300	DASI 300 or GSI
300s or **300S**	
	DASI 300s
450	DASI Hyterm 450
4013	Tek 4013 storage scope; also 4014 and 4015 without enhanced graphic module
4014 or **tek**	
	Tek 4014 and 4015 storage scope with enhanced graphic module
aed	AED 512 color
bgplot or **bitgraph**	
	BBN bitgraph
crt	crt capable of running **vi**
dumb or **un** or **unknown**	
	line printers, dumb terminals without cursor addressing
gigi or **vt125**	
	vt125
implot	Imagen
var	Benson Varian
ver	D1200A; **lpr -v** may be used to plot

All but **ver** can be used with **lpr -g** to plot

π **PMAP** — Display Address Space Map of Processes
% **/usr/proc/bin/pmap** *pids*

pids   process IDs

POSTDAISY — Diablo 630 to PostScript Translator
% **postdaisy** [*options*] [*file*]
% **/usr/lib/lp/postscript/postdaisy** [*options*] [*file*]
Option:

– c *n*	make *n* copies of each page	
– f *fname*	use font *fname* (**Courier** default)	
– h *hmi*	horizontal motion index (**12** default)	
– m *n*	magnification factor (**1.0** default)	
– n *n*	number of logical pages per physical page (**1** default)	
– o *list*	print only specified pages; ranges or comma-separated list	
– p *mode*	portrait or landscape mode (**portrait** default)	
– r *lflag*	linefeed/carriage return behavior	
	1	linefeed generates carriage return
	2	carriage return generates linefeed
	3	both **1** and **2**
– s *size*	set point size to *size*	
– v *vmi*	vertical motion index (**8** default)	
– x *xoff*	origin offset; positive means right (**0.25** inches default)	
– y *yoff*	origin offset; positive means up (**0.25** inches default)	

POSTDMD — DMD Bitmap to Postscript
% **postdmd** [*options*] [*files*]
% **/usr/lib/lp/postscript/postdmd** [*options*] [*files*]
    stdin read if **–** or no *files* specified
Options:

– b *n*	pack using *n*-byte patterns (**6** default)
– c *n*	make *n* copies of each page
– f	flip sense of bits before printing
– m *n*	magnification factor (**1.0** default)
– n *n*	number of logical pages per physical page (**1** default)
– o *list*	print only specified pages; ranges or comma-separated list
– p *mode*	portrait or landscape mode (**portrait** default)
– x *xoff*	origin offset; positive means right (**0** inches default)
– y *yoff*	origin offset; positive means up (**0** inches default)

POSTIO — Serial Interface to PostScript Printer
% **postio –l** *line* [*options*] [*files*]
% **/usr/lib/lp/postscript/postio –l** *line* [*options*] [*files*]
    stdin read if **–** or no *files* specified
Options:

– b *rate*	set specified baud rate (**9600** default)

(continued)

POSTIO, continued

−B *size*	set buffer size (**2048** bytes default)
−D	debug; log everything to **stderr**
−i	run in interactive mode (non-spool use)
−l *line*	connect to printer on *line*
−L *log*	log received data in *log* (**stdout** default)
−P *str*	send *str* to printer before printing
−q	disable status queries
−R *n*	run characteristics of **postio**
	1 single process (default)
	2 separate read and write processes
−S	slow mode (not recommended)
−t	write received data to **stdout** (non-spool use)

line   communications line to use

POSTMD — Matrix to PostScript Printer
% **postmd** [*options*] [*files*]
% **/usr/lib/lp/postscript/postmd** [*options*] [*files*]
   stdin read if − or no *files* specified
Options:

−b *n*	pack using *n*-byte patterns (**6** default)
−c *n*	make *n* copies of each page
−d *msize*	matrix dimensions; either *msize* or *ysize***x***xsize*
−g *list*	gray scale list; 255=white, 0=black
−i *list*	real number line partition list for gray scale assignment (**-1,0,1** default)
−m *n*	magnification factor (**1.0** default)
−n *n*	number of logical pages per physical page (**1** default)
−o *list*	print only specified pages; ranges or comma-separated list
−p *mode*	portrait or landscape mode (**portrait** default)
−w *y1,x1,y2,x2*	upper left and lower right of sub-matrix
−x *xoff*	origin offset; positive means right (**0** inches default)
−y *yoff*	origin offset; positive means up (**0** inches default)

POSTPLOT — Plot(4) to PostScript Translator
% **postplot** [*options*] [*files*]
% **/usr/lib/lp/postscript/postplot** [*options*] [*files*]
   stdin read if − or no *files* specified
Options:

−c *n*	make *n* copies of each page
−f *font*	print text in *font* (**Courier** default)
−m *n*	magnification factor (**1.0** default)
−n *n*	number of logical pages per physical page (**1** default)

(continued)

POSTPLOT, continued

– o *list*	print only specified pages; ranges or comma-separated list
– p *mode*	portrait or landscape mode (**landscape** default)
– w *n*	set line width to *n* points (**0** default)
– x *xoff*	origin offset; positive means right (**0** inches default)
– y *yoff*	origin offset; positive means up (**0** inches default)

POSTPRINT — Text to PostScript Translator
% **postprint** [*options*] [*files*]
% **/usr/lib/lp/postscript/postprint** [*options*] [*files*]
    stdin read if **–** or no *files* specified
Options:

– c *n*	make *n* copies of each page
– f *font*	print text in *font* (**Courier** default)
– l *n*	set page length to *n* lines (**66** default)
– m *n*	magnification factor (**1.0** default)
– n *n*	number of logical pages per physical page (**1** default)
– o *list*	print only specified pages; ranges or comma-separated list
– p *mode*	**portrait** or **landscape** mode (**portrait** default)
– r *lflag*	linefeed/carriage return behavior
	0 ignore carriage returns (default)
	1 just do carriage return
	2 carriage return generates linefeed
– s *size*	set point size to *size*
– t *n*	set tabs every *n* columns (**8** default)
– x *xoff*	origin offset; positive means right (**0.25** inches default)
– y *yoff*	origin offset; positive means up (**0.25** inches default)

POSTREVERSE — Reverse PostScript Page Order
% **postreverse** [*options*] [*file*]
% **/usr/lib/lp/postscript/postreverse** [*options*] [*file*]
    stdin read if no *file* specified
Options:

– o *list*	print only specified pages; ranges or comma-separated list
– r	don't reverse; just reformat comments

POSTTEK — Tektronix 4014 to PostScript Translator
% **posttek** [*options*] [*files*]
% **/usr/lib/lp/postscript/posttek** [*options*] [*files*]
    stdin read if **–** or no *files* specified
Options:

– c *n*	make *n* copies of each page (**1** default)
– f *font*	print text in *font* (**Courier** default)
– m *n*	magnification factor (**1.0** default)
– n *n*	number of logical pages per physical page (**1** default)

(continued)

– o *list*	print only specified pages; ranges or comma-separated list
– p *mode*	**portrait** or **landscape** mode (**landscape** default)
– w *n*	set line width to *n* points (**0** default)
– x *xoff*	origin offset; positive means right (**0** inches default)
– y *yoff*	origin offset; positive means up (**0** inches default)

PR — Print Files

% **/usr/bin/pr** [*options*] [*files*]

% **/usr/xpg4/bin/pr** [*options*] [*files*]

    stdin read if **–** or no *files* specified

Options:

– a	print multi-column output across page
– d	print double spaced
– e*cn*	expand input tabs to every *n*th position using *c* as tab char (*n*=**8** default; *c*=**tab** default)
– f	use form feed character for new page, pause before first page if **stdout** is to terminal
– F	fold input lines to fit
– h *head*	use *head* as heading line (file name default)
– i*cn*	convert whitespace to tabs every *n*th position *c* as tab char (*n*=**8** default; *c*=**tab** default)
– l*n*	set page length to *n* lines (**66** default)
– m	merge and print all *files*, one per column
+*n*	begin printing at page *n* (**1** default)
– *n*	produce *n* column output (**1** default)
– n*cn*	number lines with *n*-wide numbers followed by *c* (*n*=**5** default; *c*=**tab** default)
– o*n*	set line offset to *n* (**0** default)
– p	pause between pages if output is to a terminal
– r	no error messages if *files* cannot be opened
– s*c*	set column separator to *c* (**tab** default)
– t	don't print page heading or trailing lines
– w*n*	set line width to *n* (**72** default for equal width multi-column output, no limit otherwise)

PREX — Probe External Control

% **prex** [*options*] *cmd* [*cmd-args*]

Options:

– k	kernel mode; **– l**, **– o**, **– p** are not valid in kernel mode
– l*libs*	libs linked to the target application using **LD_PRELOAD**
– o*tfile*	set trace output file
– p*pid*	choose process by ID

(continued)

PREX, continued
  –s*max*   set maximum size in kilobytes
              of output trace file; default 4 megabytes

κ **PRINT** — Kornshell Print
% **print** [*format*] [*args*]

Options:
  –n   suppress newline
  –p   output to process spawned with **|&**
  –r   raw mode (ignore echo escapes)
  –R   ignore all further arguments than **-n**
  –s   output to history file
  –u*n*   specify file channel number (default 1)

β **PRINTENV** — Display Environment Variables
% **printenv** [*var*]

var variable to display (all default)

PRINTF — Formatted Print
% **printf** *format* [*args*]

The following escape sequences may be used:
  \a - alert signal (bell)
  \b - backspace
  \f - form feed
  \n - newline
  \r - carriage return
  \t - horizontal tab
  \v - vertical tab

format consists of text to be matched containing format
specifiers. A format specifier has the form:
  %<*flags*><*width*><**.***prec*>**s**

<*flags*> zero or more of:
  –   left justify within field
  0   leading zero pad

<*width*> maximum field width (optional)
<*prec*> precision (optional, precede with .)
    maximum chars from *arg*

args are strings to be formatted and printed

PRIOCNTL — Process Scheduler Control
% **priocntl** −**l**
    display class configuration information
% **priocntl** −**d** [−**i** *type*] [*idlist*]
    display scheduling information about
    specified processes
% **priocntl** −**e** [−**c** *class*] [*classopt*] *command* [*args*]
    execute *command* with specified priority
% **priocntl** −**s** [−**c** *class*] [*classopt*] [−**i** *type*] [*list*]
    set scheduling priority of specified processes

Options:
−**c** *class*	class of processes; if not specified		
	must select processes all in one class		
		RT	real time
		TS	time sharing
−**i** *type*	process type (**pid** default)		
		all	all processes
		class	**RT** or **TS** in *idlist*
			defaults to −**c** class or class of
			selected process's current class
		gid	*idlist* contains group IDs
		pgid	*idlist* contains process group IDs
		pid	*idlist* contains process IDs
		ppid	*idlist* contains parent process IDs
		sid	*idlist* contains session IDs
		uid	*idlist* contains effective user IDs

idlist	list of IDs of type specified by −**i** option
	default is related ID of **priocntl** command itself
class_opt	class specific options
−**m** *lim*	set user priority limit to *lim* (TS only)
−**p** *pri*	set processes' priority to *pri*
−**t** *quan* [−**r** *res*]	
	set time quantum to *quan*
	res is fraction of second resolution
	(**1000** default) (RT only)

PROF — Display Profile Data
% **prof** [*options*] [*file*]
    a.out used if no *file* specified
Options:
−**a**	sort by increasing symbol address
−**c**	sort by decreasing number of calls
−**C**	demangle C++ function and variable
	names before printing
−**g**	include static functions
−**h**	don't print report heading
−**l**	don't include static functions (default)
−**m** *profile*	name of profile data source
	(**mon.out** default)
−**n**	sort lexically by symbol name
−**o**	print symbol address in octal with name
−**s**	print summary on **stderr**

(continued)

PROF, continued

−t	sort by decreasing percentage of total time (default)
−V	print version information
−x	print symbol address in hex with name
−z	include symbols even if zero calls and time

PRS — Print Parts of SCCS Files
% **prs** [*options*] *files*
    SCCS filenames read from **stdin** if *files* is −
Options:

−a	include removed deltas
−c[*date*]	cutoff date and time in format *YY*[*MM*[*DD*[*HH*[*MM*[*SS*]]]]]
−d[*text*]	output specification (includes data keys)
−e	include deltas at *sid* or *date* and earlier (see **−c** or **−r**)
−l	include deltas at *sid* or *date* and later (see **−c** or **−r**)
−r[*sid*]	specify SCCS ID of version (top delta default)

PRT — Display SCCS Delta History
% **prt** [*options*] *files*
Options:

−a	include removed deltas
−b	print body of SCCS file
−c[*date*]	cutoff date and time in format *YY*[*MM*[*DD*[*HH*[*MM*[*SS*]]]]] (**0000 GMT 01/01/70** default)
−d	print type delta table entries
−e	equivalent to **−dfitu**
−f	print flags
−i	print serial numbers of deltas
−r[*date*]	like **−c** but selects older than cutoff time (nothing printed in no *date*)
−s	print only first line of delta entries
−t	print descriptive text
−u	print logins and/or groups of users
−y[*sid*]	print deltas up to *sid* (only first if no *sid* specified) allowed to make deltas

π **PRUN** — Set Processes Running
% **/usr/proc/bin/prun** *pids*

pids	process IDs

PS — Report Process Status
% **ps** [*options*]
Options:

−a	print all processes except session leaders and non-terminal associated
−A	print info for all processes
−c	include scheduler priorities
−d	print all processes except session leaders

(continued)

PS, continued

– e	print all processes
– f	print full listing
– g *list*	list only processes whose leaders are in *list*
– G *list*	list only processes whose group IDs are in *list*
– j	print session & process group ID
– l	long listing (more info than **– f**)
– n *namlst*	for compatability only; ignored
– o *fmt*	specify display format *fmt* may be any one of: **F, S, UID, PID, PPID, C CLS, PRI, NI, ADDR, SZ, WCHAN, STIME, TTY, TIME, CMD, PGID, SID**
– p *list*	list only processes whose IDs are in *list*
– s *list*	list info about session leaders in *list*
– t *list*	list only processes of terminals in *list*
– u *list*	list only processes with effective user IDs in *list*
– U *list*	list only processes with real user IDs in *list*
list	comma or blank-separated list with optional enclosing double quotes

β **PS** — Report Process Status

% **/usr/ucb/ps** [*options*] [*pid*]

if no *options*, print info about processes associated with controlling terminal

Options:

– a	all 'interesting' processes
– c	display command name from system info
– g	all processes
– l	long listing
– n	numerical output in WCHAN and USER fields
– r	only print running and runnable processes
– S	display accumulated CPU time
– t*term*	list processes associated with terminal *term*
– u	user-oriented output
– U	update **ps** private database
– v	display virtual memory info
– w	132 column output (**80** default)
– ww	arbitrary width output
– x	include processes with no controlling terminal

pid restrict output to process *pid*

π **PSIG** — Display Signal Actions of Processes

% **/usr/proc/bin/psig** *pids*

pids   process IDs

π **PSTACK** — Display Stack Traces for Processes

% **/usr/proc/bin/pstack** *pids*

(continued)

PSTACK, continued
pids   process IDs

π **PSTOP** — Stop Processes
% **/usr/proc/bin/pstop** pids

pids   process IDs

π **PTIME** — Display /proc Status Info
% **/usr/proc/bin/ptime** cmd [args]

cmd   a command to time
args   arguments to the timed command

π **PTREE** — Display Process Trees
% **/usr/proc/bin/ptree** [[pid | user]...]

pid process ID
user   user name

PVS — Show Dynamic Objects Invertal Version Info
% **pvs** [options] files
Options:
     – d   print version definition info
     – n   normalize version def info
     – Nnam   print only info for given
                     version definition name
     – o   print single line definitions
     – r   print version dependency
                     (requirements) info
     – s   print symbols for version definitions
     – v   verbose

π **PWAIT** — Wait for Processes to Terminate
% **/usr/proc/bin/pwait** [- **v**] pids
Option:
     – v   verbose

pids   process IDs

PWD — Print Working Directory Name
% **/usr/bin/pwd**

π **PWDX** — Display Working Directory of Processes
% **/usr/proc/bin/pwdx** pids

pids   process IDs

RCP — Remote File Copy
% **rcp** [option] file1 file2
     copy from file1 to file2
Option:
     – p   attempt to preserve modify and
                     access times

(continued)

RCP, continued

% **rcp** [*options*] *files dir*
   copy *files* to directory *dir*

Options:

−p	attempt to preserve modify and access times
−r	copy each subtree rooted at *file*

RDIST — Remote File Distribution

% **rdist** [*options*] **−c** *paths*
% **rdist** [*options*] *package*

Options:

−b	binary comparison
−c *paths*	update *paths* on named host
−d *macro=value*	
	assign *value* to *macro*
−D	enable debug mode
−f *distfile*	use *distfile* as description file (− indicates standard input)
−h	follow symbolic links; copy file, not link itself
−i	ignore unresolved links
−m *host*	limit update to machine *host* (multiple **−m** permitted)
−n	print commands but don't execute
−q	don't show files being updated
−R	remove extraneous files
−v	verify files are up to date on all hosts
−w	append whole file name to destination directoryOK
−y	don't update remote copies younger than master; issue warning

READ — Read Utility

% **/usr/bin/read** [**-r**] [*vars*]

Option:

−r	treat backslash as normal character

vars variables name to receive input data

κ **READ** — KornShell Read

% **read** [*options*] [*name***?***prompt*] [*names*]

Options:

−p	read input from pipe of process started with **|&**
−r	treat backslash as normal character
−s	input saved as command in history file
−u *n*	read from input channel *n*

names	variable names to receive input data
prompt	prompt printed to **stderr** for input

σ **READ** — Shell Read

% **read** [*names*]

names	variable name to receive input data
prompt	prompt printed to **stderr** for input

ϕ **READFILE** — Read File and Copy to **stdout**
% **readfile** *file*
    longest line info saved for subsequent call to
    longline

RED — Restricted Version of **ed** Text Editor
% **red** [*options*] [*file*]
See **ED** command for description of options and
Page 2 for list of commands

REFER — Insert from Bibliographic Database
% **refer** [*options*] *files*
Option:

− **a**[*n*]	reverse the first *n* author names (all names default)
− **b**	don't put flags in text
− **c**str	capitalize (small caps) fields whose key-letters are in *str*
− **e**	accumulate references until following sequence encountered .[$LIST$.]
− **k**[*x*]	instead of numbering lines, use key labels as specified in reference data line beginning with %*x* (**%L** default)
− **l**[*m*][**,***n*]	instead of numbering references, labels are formed from first *m* letters of last name and last *n* digits of date (entire item default)
− **n**	don't search default file
− **p** [*file*]	search *file* for references before default file
− **s**[*str*]	sort references by fields whose key-letters are in *str* (**AD** Default)

REGCMP — Compile Regular Expression
% **regcmp** [*option*] *files*
    compile regular expression in *file* into *file*.**i**
Option:

−	place output in *file*.**c** instead of *file*.**i**

ϕ **REGEX** — Match Patterns Against String
% **regex** [*options*] [*re template*] *re* [*template*]
Options:

− **e**	evaluate corresponding template and write result to **stdout**
− **v** [*str*]	use *str* to match against *re*s instead of **stdin**
re	regular expression to match against
template	template to return on match if the last *template* is omitted, a match will return TRUE **$m0** through **$m9** in template refer to (. . .)**$0** through (. . .)**$9** in *re*

ξ **REHASH** — Recompute Internal Hash Table
% **rehash**

ϕ **REINIT** — Run Initialization File
% **reinit** *file*

REMSH — Remote Shell
(remsh is an alias for rsh, see **rsh**)

RENICE — Alter Priority of Running Processes
% **renice** [*option*] *pid*
% **renice** *priority* [*option*]
Option:

– g*gid*	specify group IDs *gid*
– n*n*	specify priority increment of *n*
– p*pid*	specify process IDs *pid*
– u*user*	specify user IDs as name *user*
– u*uid*	specify user IDs as numerical *uid*

κ **READONLY** — Preclude Shell Variable From
    Reassignment
% **readonly** *defs*

defs[*var* [=*val*]]
var   variable to be defined
val   value of variable

σ **READONLY** — Preclude Shell Variable From
    Reassignment
See **Built-in Commands** in the Solaris SHELL section
Pages 168-172

ξ **REPEAT** — Looping Command
% **repeat** *count command*

RESET — Reset Terminal Characteristics
% **reset**
you may need to surround **reset** with linefeed characters
Note: all **tset** options can be used with **reset**

ϕ **RESET** — Reset Form Field to Defaults
% **reset**

$\kappa\sigma$ **RETURN** — Return to Calling Shell
% **return** [*n*]

RKSH — Restricted Korn Shell (See **KSH**)
% **/usr/bin/rksh** [*options*] [*args*]

RLOGIN — Remote Login
% **rlogin** [*options*] *hostname*
Options:

– 8	use 8-bit data
– e*c*	set escape character to *c* (~ default)
– l *user*	use *user* as remote login name
– L	allow session to run in litout mode

RM — Remove Files
% **/usr/bin/rm** [*options*] *files*
% **/usr/xpg4/bin/rm** [*options*] *files*
Options:

– f	force removal of files without write permission
– i	ask for confirmation before each delete
– r	recursively delete directories
– R	same as **– r**

RMAIL — Restricted Mail
% **rmail** [*options*] *users*

– m *mtype*	add **Message-Type:** *mtype*
– t	include list of people **mail** sent to in **To:** lines
– w	don't wait for completion of remote transfer program to send to remote user

RMDEL — Remove an SCCS Delta Version
% **/usr/ccs/bin/rmdel – r***sid files*
SCCS filenames read from **stdin** if *files* is –
Argument:

– r*sid*	specify SCCS ID of version to be removed

RMDIR — Remove Empty Directories (See **RM**)
% **/usr/bin/rmdir** [*options*] *directories*
Options:

– p	remove empty parent directories
– s	suppress error messages

ROFFBIB — Format Bibliographic Database
% **roffbib** [*options*] [*files*]
stdin read if no *files* specified
Options:

– e	equally spaced words in justified lines
– h	speed output with tabs (set every 8 spaces)
– m *name*	prepend macro file **/usr/share/lib/tmac/tmac.***name* replaces macros defined in **/usr/share/lib/tmac/tmac.bib**
– n*n*	number first page *n*
– o*list*	print only listed page numbers
– Q	queue output for typesetter; page offset set to 1 inch
– r*an*	set number register *a* to *n* (*a* is one character only)
– s[*n*]	stop every n pages (**1** default)
– T*name*	specify output device type
– V	send output to Versatec, page offset 1 inch
– x	don't print abstracts
list	comma-separated, *n–m* is range, *–n* is beginning to page *n*, *n–* is page *n* to end

RPCGEN — RPC Protocol Compiler
% **rpcgen** [*options*] [*file*]
    stdin read if no *file* specified
Options:

−**a**	generate all files	
−**A**	enable automatic MT mode	
−**b**	backward compatibility mode	
−**C**	generate ANSI C stubs and headers	
−**D***name*[**=val**]		
	define *name* to *val* (**null** default)	
−**i***size*	size at which to generate inline code (**5** default)	
−**K** *n*	set wait before exit time to *n* seconds (**120** default; use **0** for immediate exit, **−1** for never exit)	
−**L**	server logs to **syslog** instead of **stderr**	
−**N**	allow multiple arguments to procedures	
−**n** *netid*	compile into server side stubs for transport specified by *netid*	
−**o** *output*	specify name of output file (valid with −*outdef* only)	
−*outdef*	selective output (all files default) outdef is one of:	
	c	compile into XDR routines
	h	compile into C header file
	l	compile into client side stubs
	m	compile into server side stubs
	M	generate multi-thread safe stubs
	n *netid*	compile into server side stubs for transport *netid*
	s *nettype*	
		compile into server side stubs for transports of class *nettype*
	t	compile into RPC dispatch table
−**Sc**	generate sample client code	
−**Sm**	generate sample **Makefile**	
−**Ss**	generate sample server code	
−**T**	generate code to support RPC dispatch tables	
−**Y** *dirpath*	look for C preprocessor in *dirpath*	

RSH — Remote Shell
(remsh is an alias for rsh)
% **rsh** [*options*] *hostname* [*command*]
% **rsh** *hostname* [*options*] [*command*]
% *hostname* [*options*] [*command*]
Options:

−**l** *user*	use *user* as the remote username (local user name default)
−**n**	redirect input of **rsh** from **/dev/null**

If **rsh** is invoked by any name other than **rsh** it assumes the invocation name is a hostname.

ϕ **RUN** — RUN Executable
% **run** [*options*] *program*
Options:
    −e   prompt if error before returning to FMLI
    −n   never prompt before returning to FMLI
    −s   screen, repaint not required
    −t *string*   *string* is name for menu process

RUP — Display Host Status of Remote Machines
% **rup** [*options*]
    broadcast query and display responses
Options:
    −h   sort by host name
    −l   sort by load average
    −t   sort by up time
% **rup** [*hosts*]
    only query specified hosts

RUPTIME — Report Status of Local Machines
% **ruptime** [*options*]
Options:
    −a   include idle users in count
    −l   sort by load average
    −r   reverse sort order
    −t   sort by up time
    −u   sort by number of users

β **RUSAGE** — Display Resource Usage of Command
% **r/usr/ucb/rusage** *command*
    run *command* and display system resource usage

RUSERS — Remote **who**
% **rusers** [*options*] *hosts*
Options:
    −a   report machine even if no active users
    −h   sort output by hostname
    −i   sort by idle time
    −l   long list
    −u   sort by number of users

RWHO — Who is On Local Machines
% **rwho** [*option*]
Option:
    −a   include idle users in count

SACT — Print SCCS File Editing Activity
% **sact** *files*
    SCCS filenames read from **stdin** if files is −

SAG — Graphically Display **sar** Data
% **sag** [*options*]
Options:

−e *time*	select data up to *time* (**18:00** default)
−f *file*	use file for input (**/usr/adm/sa/sa**dd for current day default)
−i *sec*	select data at *sec* intervals
−s *time*	select data later than *time* (**08:00** default)
−T *term*	format output for *term* (env variable **TERM** default)
−x *spec*	x axis specification in form:

                   name [*op name*] ... [*lo hi*]

                   name   **+**, **-**, *****, or **/** delimited by blank space

                   lo hi   numeric scale limits

    −y *spec*   as with X axis spec but up to 5 can be included, separated by a ;

SAR — System Activity Reporter
% **sar** [*options*] *t* [*n*]
Options:

−a	report use of file access system routines
−A	report all data
−b	report buffer activity
−c	report system calls
−d	report block device activity
−e *time*	select data up to *time*
−f *file*	use *file* as data source default is **/usr/adm/sa/sa**dd
−g	report paging activities
−i *sec*	data at intervals close to *sec* seconds
−k	report kernel memory allocation activities
−m	report message and semaphore activities
−o *file*	save samples to *file* in binary format
−p	report paging activities
−q	report average queuing length while occupied and percent of time occupied
−r	report unused memory and storage
−s *time*	select data later than *time*
−u	report cpu utilization (default)
−v	report status of process, inode, and file tables
−w	report system swapping and switching activities
−y	report tty device activity

t   number of intervals in *t* seconds
r   number of seconds used to measure intervals

SCCS — Source Code Control System
  See **admin**, **cdc**, **comb**, **delta**, **get**, **prs**, **prt**, **rmdel**,
  sact, **sccsdiff**, **unget**, **val**, and **what**

% **/usr/ccs/bin/sccs** [*options*] *sccs_cmd* [*sccs_flags*]
Options:
  − **d***pprefix*   path prefix (current directory default)
  − **p***psuffix*   path suffix (SCCS default)
  − **r**   run sccs as real user, not SCCS effective
              uid

SCCSDIFF — SCCS Version Difference
% **/usr/ccs/bin/sccsdiff** − **r***sid1* − **r***sid2* [*options*] *files*
Options:
  − **p**   format output using **pr**
  − **r***s*   specify delta for comparison
  (**DIFF** options are also available)

SCRIPT — Make Log Of Terminal Session
% **script** [*option*] [*outfile*]
  output to **typescript** if no *outfile* specified
Option:
  − **a**   append to *outfile*

SDIFF — Side-By-Side Difference
% **sdiff** [*options*] *file1 file2*
Options:
  − **l**   print only identical lines on left side
  − **o** *file*   merge *file1* and *file2* to *file*, identical
              lines are passed directly, else user
              prompted:
      e   edit an empty file
      e b   edit both left and right columns
      e l   edit left column
      e r   edit right column
      l   append left column
      q   exit
      r   append right column
      s   suppress printing of identical
                lines
      v   enable printing of identical lines
  − **s**   suppress printing of identical lines
  − **w** *n*   set width of output line to *n* (**130** default)

SED — Stream Editor
% **/usr/bin/sed** [*options*] [*files*]
% **/usr/xpg4/bin/sed** [*options*] [*files*]
% **sed** [*options*] [*files*]
  stdin read if no *files* specified
Options:
  − **e** *script*   editor commands in *script* executed
  − **f** *file*   editor commands read from *file*
  − **n**   suppress unrequested output

(continued)

SED, continued

Command Format:
    [*addr1* [,*addr2*]] *function* [*args*]
Addresses

.	current line
$	last line
n	*n*th line
/*re*/	next line with /*re*/
crec	as above using *c* as delimiter

(See Page 173 for Regular Expressions)

\n	matches newline embedded in pattern space

no specified address matches all lines
one address matches only matching lines
two addresses select inclusive range

Commands:
(number in ( ) is number of addresses); the
number and ( ) should not be entered

(0)	empty commands are ignored
(0)**#**	if **#** is first character, treat entire line as comment
(1)**a**\ *text*	append; end with period alone on a line
(2)**b** *label*	branch :*label*
(2)**c**\ *text*	change pattern space
(2)**d**	delete pattern space
(2)**D**	delete first line of pattern space
(2)**g**	replace pattern space with hold space
(2)**G**	append pattern space to hold space
(2)**h**	replace hold space with pattern space
(2)**H**	append hold space to pattern space
(1)**i**\ *text*	insert *text* before current line
(2)**l**	list pattern space on **stdout** "spells out" control characters
(2)**n**	copy pattern space to **stdout**
(2)**N**	append next input line to pattern space with embedded newline
(2)**p**	print pattern space on **stdout**
(2)**P**	print first line of pattern space on **stdout**
(1)**q**	quit by branching to end of script
(1)**r** *file*	read contents of *file*
(2)**s**/*re*/*nre*/*flgs*	substitute *nre* for *re*
	flgs are:
	g globally (non-overlapping)
	n substitute in just *n* occurrence
	p print pattern space if replacement was made
	w *file* write pattern space to *file* if replacement was made
(2)**t** *label*	branch to :*label* if substitutions made
(2)**w** *file*	write pattern space to *file*
(2)**x**	exchange pattern and hold space

(continued)

SED, continued

    (2)**y/**_str1_**/**_str2_**/**

                replace _str1_ with _str2_;
                strings must be of equal length

    (2)**!** _func_   apply _func_ to addresses not selected

    (0)**:** _label_   label for **b** and **t** commands

    (1)**=**   write current line number to **stdout**

    (2)**{**   execute commands through **}** if pattern
                space is selected

#n as first line is same as **– n** option (suppress
default output); treat rest of line after **#n** as comment

Note: the **/** in the **s** and **y** commands can be
replaced with any character

β **SED** — Stream Editor
% **sed** [_options_] [_files_]
See native sed command for description of options

ξ **SET** — Set C Shell Variable
% **set** [_var_ [= _value_]]
% **set** _var_[_n_] [= _value_]]
% **set** _var_ = **$<**

var	variable to be assigned
value	value of variable

κ **SET** — Set KornShell Variables
% **set** [_options_] [_args_]
Options:

– A	array assignment
+ A	array assignment, variable not unset first
– a	all subsequent variables are exported
– e	conditions execution of **ERR** trap
– f	disables file name generation
– h	each command becomes a tracked alias
– k	all variable assignment arguments in environment
– m	background jobs run in separate process group
– n	check commands but do not execute
– o	set any of:

                allexport
                    same as -a
                errexit same as -e
                bgnice background jobs run at lower
                    priority
                gmacs gmacs style command line editing
                ignoreeof
                    shell doesn't exit on EOF
                keyword
                    same as -k
                markdirs
                    file name generated directory
                    names have appended slash (**/**)
                monitor
                    same as -m

(continued)

> > **noclobber**
> >
> > > prevents > from truncating
> > > existing files; truncate then
> > > requires >|
> >
> > **noexec** same as -n
> > **noglob** same as -f
> > **nolog** don't save function definitions in
> > history file
> > **nounset**
> >
> > > same as -u
> >
> > **privileged**
> >
> > > same as -p
> >
> > **verbose**
> >
> > > same as -v
> >
> > **trackall**
> >
> > > same as -h
> >
> > **vi** vi like command line editing
> > **viraw** each character processed as in **vi**
> > **xtrace** same as -x

– p	disable processing of **$HOME/.profile**
– s	sort positional parameters
– t	exit after one command
– u	error on unset parameters when substituting
– v	print shell input lines as read
– x	print commands and arguments as they are executed
–	turn off **-x** and **-v** flags and stops examining arguments for flags
--	change no flags

ϕ **SET** — Set Environment Variable
% **set** [*options*]
Options:

    – e *var*[=*val*]
            set *var* in UNIX environment
    – f*file var*[=*val*]
            set *var* in global environment; *file*
            contains lines of form *var=val*
    – l *var*[=*val*]
            set *var* in local environment

σ **SET** — Set Shell Variables
% **set** [*options*] [*args*]
Options:

– a	all subsequent variables are exported
– e	exit immediately if a command exits with non-zero result
– f	disables file name generation
– h	locate and remember function commands as defined
– k	all variable assignment arguments in environment
– n	check commands but do not execute
– t	exit after one command

(continued)

SET, continued

−u	error on unset parameters when substituting
−v	print shell input lines as read
−x	print commands and arguments as they are executed
−‑	change no flags

ϕ **SETCOLOR** — Redefine or Create Color
% **setcolor** *color redlevel greenlevel bluelevel*
    defines the makeup of *color* with intensity values
    from **0** to **1000**

ξ **SETENV** — Set C Shell Environment Variable
% **setenv** [*VAR* [*word*]]

VAR	environment variable to be defined
word	value of environment variable

SETFACL — Modify ACLs
% **setfacl** [*options*] *acl_entries files*
% **setfacl** [*options*] *acl_file files*
Options:

−d *acl_entries*	
	delete entries from file
−f*acl_file*	set entries with input from *acl_file*
−m *acl_entries*	
	add new entries
−r	recalculate permissions for file group class entry
−s *acl_entries*	
	set acl

σ **SH** — Shell (See also: Pages 168-172)
% **/usr/bin/sh** [*options*] [*args*]
% **/usr/xpg4/bin/sh** [*options*] [*args*]
(**/usr/xpg4/bin/sh** is identical to **/usr/bin/ksh**; see **KSH**)
(**/usr/bin/jsh** is **/usr/bin/sh** with Job Control turned on)
Options:

− −	don't change any flags (useful to set **$1** to **−**)
−a	mark modified export variables
−c *cmd*	execute *cmd* (default reads commands from file named in first entry of *args*)
−e	if non-interactive, exit if a command fails
−f	disable wildcarding
−h	locate and remember functions on definition instead of on execution
−i	set interactive mode
−k	all keyword arguments placed in environment
−n	read commands without executing them
−p	don't set effective IDs to real IDs
−r	set restricted mode
−s	read commands from **stdin**
−t	read and execute one command then exit

(continued)

SH, continued
- **−u**   set error upon substituting an unset variable
- **−v**   print input lines as read
- **−x**   print commands with arguments as executed

ϕ **SHELL** — Run Shell Command
% **shell** *commands*
(defaults to use **/usr/bin/sh** unless **$SHELL** set)

ξ **SHIFT** — Shift Variable Array by One
% **shift** [*variable*]

$\kappa\sigma$ **SHIFT** — Shift Array Stack
% **shift** [*n*]

SIZE — Size of Object File
% **size** [*options*] [*files*]
Options:
- **−f**   include details on each section
- **−F**   include details on each segment
- **−n**   include data on non-loadable segments or non-allocatable sections
- **−o**   print number in octal (decimal default)
- **−V**   print **size** version number on **stderr**
- **−x**   print number in hexadecimal

SLEEP — Suspend Execution for Specified Duration
% **sleep** *seconds*

SOELIM — Resolve **.so** Requests
% **soelim** [*files*]
     stdin read if − or no *files* specified

SORT — Sort/Merge Files
% **/usr/bin/sort** [*options*] [*files*]
% **/usr/xpg4/bin/sort** [*options*] [*files*]
     stdin read if − or no *files* specified
Options:
- **−b**   ignore leading tabs and spaces
- **−c**   check that input is in sorted order
- **−d**   dictionary order (use only letters, digits, tabs, and spaces)
- **−f**   sort upper case and lower case together
- **−i**   ignore non-printables in comparisons
- **−k** *field_start* [**type**] [**,field_end**] [**type**]   alternate key field definition
- **−m**   merge already sorted *files*
- **−M**   compare as months (implies **−b**)
- **−n**   numeric sort (implies **−b**)
- **−o** *output*   place sorted results in *output*
- **−r**   reverse sort; descending order
- **−t***c*   set field separator to *c* (**tab** default)
- **−T***dir*   place temporary files in *dir*
- **−u**   output only one occurrence of duplicate lines

(continued)

SORT, continued

    – y[*mem*]   kbytes of memory to start with,
                 0 = minimum. no arg = maximum
    – z[*size*]   bytes in longest line read
                 (obsolete)
    +*pos1* [– *pos2*]

                 sort only from *pos1* to *pos2*; if *pos2* not
                 specified, key includes up to the end of
                 line
                 pos1 and *pos2* of the form: $m[.n]$[**bdfiMnr**])
                 m   *m* fields from start of line skipped
                        (**0** default)
                 n   *n* characters from start of field
                        skipped (**0** default)
                 bdfiMnr
                        option applies only to
                        specified key

SORTBIB — Sort Bibliographic Database
% **sortbib** *option database*
Options:
    – s *keyltrs*   sort by specified key letters

SOURCE — Scan/Execute Commands
% **source** [- **h**] *name*
Options:
    – h   place command in history file instead
                 of executing them

SPELL — Find Spelling Errors
% **spell** [*options*] [*files*]
    stdin read if no *files* specified
Options:
    +*local*   remove all words found in *local*
                 from output
    – b   check British spelling
    – i   cause deroff to ignore .so and .nx
                 commands
    – v   print words not literally in list and
                 derivations
    – x   print stems for each word

SPLINE — Interpolate Smooth Curve
% **spline** [*options*] num_pairs
Options:
    – a [*n*]   abscissas not in data, use *n* as
                 spacing (1 default)
    – k [*n*]   set k in boundary equation
                 to *n* (**0** default)
    – *n*   space output points *n* intervals
                 between lower and upper **x** limits
                 (**100** default)
    – p   make output periodic
    – x *low* [*high*]

                 specify lower (and upper) bounds;
                 automatic abscissas start at *low*

(continued)

SPLINE, continued
num_pairs   abscissas and ordinates of function to
                     plot or just ordinates if **− a** specified

SPLIT — Break File into Pieces
% **split** [*option*] [*file* [*name*]]
    stdin read if **−** or no *file* specified
Options:
    − n   set size of split files to *n* lines
                     (**1000** default)
    − a *suffixlen*
                     use *suffixlen* letters to form suffix part
                     of filenames of the split file
    − b *n*   split file into pieces n bytes in size
    − b *n***k** split file into pieces n kilobytes in size
    − b *n***m** split file into pieces n megabytes in size
    − l *n*   set size of split files to *n* lines
                     (**1000** default)
    name   output *name***aa**, *name***ab**, ... (**xaa** default)

SRCHTXT — Search Message Data Bases
% **srchtxt** [*options*] [*text*]
Options:
    − l *locale* access files in
                     /usr/lib/locale/*locale***/LC_MESSAGES**
    − m *msgfile*
                     access specified *msgfile* which can be
                     a comma-delimited list. Leading **/**
                     indicates pathname else assume directory
                     /usr/lib/locale/*locale***/LC_MESSAGES**
    − s   suppress printing of message numbers

text   string or regular expression to be searched for

If not otherwise specified, *locale* is determined by the
value of the **LC_MESSAGES** or the **LANG**
environment variable

*ξκσ***STOP** — Stop Execution of Background Jobs
See **Job Control** in Solaris SHELL section Pages 168-172

STRCHG — Change Streams Configuration
% **strchg − h** *module1*[**,***module2* ...]
    push modules onto stream
% **strchg − f** *file*
    configure stream with modules specified in *file*
% **strchg − p** [*options*]
    pop module from stream
Options:
    − a   pop all modules above topmost driver
    − u *module* pop all modules above *module*

STRCONF — Print List of Modules In A Stream
% **strconf** [*option*]
Options:

    – m *module*

                determine if *module* is in stream

    –t   print name of topmost module only

STRINGS — Search Binary Files for ASCII Strings
% **strings** [*options*] *files*
Options:

– a	search beyond initialized data space
–n *n*	use *n* as minimum string length (**4** default)
–o	print octal offset in file for each string
–t*fmt*	print string preceded by its byte offset from the start of the file (*fmt* (**d, o, x**))

STRIP — Remove Symbol Table and Relocation Bits
% **/usr/ccs/bin/strip** [*options*] *files*
Options:

– l	strip line number info only
– V	print version information
– x	don't strip external or static symbol info

STTY — Set Terminal Options
% **stty** [**– a**] [**– g**] [*options*]
% **STTY** [**– a**] [**– g**] [*options*]
Options:

– a	print all option settings
– g	print settings in **stty** argument format
0	hang up phone line
async	set normal async mode with clock modes **xcibrg**, **rcibrg**, **tsetcoff** and **rsetcoff**
[**–]brkint**	[do not] send **INTR** signal on input break
bs*n*	set output delay after backspace (**0** or **1**)
[**–]cdxon**	[disable]/enable CD output flow control
[**–]clocal**	[enable]/disable modem control
cols *n*	same as **columns** *c*
columns *n*	set window to *n* columns
cooked	disable raw input & output (same as **– raw**)
[**–]cread**	[disable]/enable receiver
cr*n*	set output delay after carriage return (**0** to **3**)
cs*n*	set character size to *n* bits (**5** to **8**)
[**–]crtscts**	[disable]/enable RTS modem control lines
[**–]cstopb**	set [one]/two stop bits per character
ctab *c*	set CTAB char to *c* (used with **–stappl**)
[**–]ctsxon**	[disable]/enable CTS output flow control
discard *c*	set "discard output" character to *c* (^**O** default)

(continued)

127

dsusp c	generate SIGTSTP signal when foreground process group attempts to read c (`Y default)
[-]**dtrxoff**	[disable]/enable DTR input flow control
[-]**echo**	[do not] echo all input characters
[-]**echoctl**	[do not] echo control chars as ^char
[-]**echoe**	[do not] echo **ERASE** for CRTs
[-]**echok**	[do not] echo a newline after **KILL**
[-]**echoke**	[do not] BS-SP-BS erase line on line kill
[-]**echonl**	[do not] echo newlines
[-]**echoprt**	[do not] echo erase char as char is "erased"
ek	reset **ERASE** to # and **KILL** to @
eof c	set end of file character to c (^D default)
eol c	set line delimiter to c
eol2 c	set additional line delimiter to c
erase c	set character **ERASE** character to c (# default)
[-]**evenp**	same as [-]**parenb** and **cs[8]**/7
ff$n$	set output delay after form-feed (**0** or **1**)
[-]**flusho**	[do not]/flush output buffers
[-]**hup**	[do not]/do hang up on last close
[-]**hupcl**	same as **hup**
[-]**icanon**	[disable]/enable checking for **ERASE** and **KILL**
[-]**icrnl**	[do not] map CR to NL on input
[-]**iexten**	[disable]/enable extended input functions
[-]**ignbrk**	[do not] ignore break on input
[-]**igncr**	[do not] ignore CR on input
[-]**ignpar**	[do not] ignore parity errors
[-]**imaxbel**	
	[do not] echo BEL when input too long
[-]**inlcr**	[do not] map input newline to carriage return
[-]**inpck**	[disable]/enable input parity check
intr c	set **INTR** (interrupt) character to c (DEL default)
[-]**isig**	[disable]/enable checking for **INTR**, **SWTCH** and **QUIT**
ispeed n	set input baud rate to n (**0** indicates **ispeed** is to be set to **ospeed**
[-]**istrip**	[do not] strip 8th bit of input characters
[-]**isxoff**	[disable]/enable isochronous input flow control
[-]**iuclc**	[do not] map input upper case to lower case
[-]**ixany**	allow [**XON**]/any character to restart **XOFF**
[-]**ixoff**	[disable]/enable **XON/XOFF** during input
[-]**ixon**	[disable]/enable **XON/XOFF** protocol
kill c	set line **KILL** character to c (@ default)
[-]**lcase**	same as [-]**xcase**, [-]**iuclc**, and [-]**olcuc**
[-]**LCASE**	same as [-]**lcase**
line n	set line discipline to n (**1** to **126** allowed)

(continued)

lnext *c*	use *c* to escape special meaning of next char (`˜V` default)
[–]**loblk**	[do not] block input from non-current layer
min *c*	set **MIN** value to *c* (used with **– icanon**)
[–]**markp**	[disable]/enable **parenb**, **cs7**/[**cs8**], **parodd** and **parext**
n	set terminal baud rate to *n*
[–]**nl**	same as [**icrnl**]/**– icrnl** and [**onlcr**]/**– onlcr** [and **– inlcr**, **– igncr**, **– ocrnl**, and **– onlret**]
nl*n*	set output delay after newline (**0** or **1**)
[–]**noflsh**	[do not] no flush after **INTR** or **QUIT** or **SWTCH**
[–]**ocrnl**	[do not] map output carriage return to newline
[–]**oddp**	same as [–]**parenb**, [–]**parodd**, and **cs**[**8**]/7
[–]**ofdel**	set fill character to [**NUL**]/**DEL**
[–]**ofill**	delay output with [timing]/fill characters
[–]**olcuc**	[do not] map output lower case to upper case
[–]**onlcr**	[do not] map output newline to carriage return
[–]**onlret**	terminal does [not] carriage return after newline
[–]**onocr**	[do]/don't output carriage return at column 0
[–]**opost**	[do not] post-process output
ospeed *n*	set output baud rate to *n* (**0** causes an immediate hangup)
[–]**parenb**	[disable]/enable parity detection & generation
[–]**parext**	[disable]/enable checking for mark and space parity
[–]**parity**	same as [–]**parenb** and **cs**[**8**]/7
[–]**parmrk**	[do not] mark parity errors
[–]**parodd**	select [even]/odd parity
[–]**pendin**	[do not] retype pending input at next read
quit *c*	set **QUIT** character to *c* (`˜l` default)
[–]**raw**	[disable]/enable raw input and output
rcibrg	use internal baud generator for rec clock
rcrset	use EIA-232-D pin 17 as xmit clock
rctset	use EIA-232-D pin 15 as xmit clock
reprint *c*	*c* will cause all unread characters to be reprinted (`˜R` default)
rows *n*	set window size to *n* rows
rsetcoff	rec clock not provided
rsetcrbrg	output rec baud rate generator on CCITT V.24, ckt. 128
rsetctbrg	output xmit baud rate generator on CCITT V.24, ckt. 128
rsetcrset	output RC on CCITT V.24, ckt. 128
rsetctset	output TC on CCITT V.24, ckt. 128
[–]**rtsxoff**	[disable]/enable RTS input flow control
sane	reset all modes to "sane" values
[–]**spacep**	[disable]/enable **parenb**, **cs7** and **parext**

(continued)

STTY, continued

[–]**stappl**	use application/[line] mode on sync. line
start *c*	use *c* to resume output (^Q default)
[–]**stflush**	enable/[disable] **flush** after **write**
stop *c*	use *c* to suspend output (^S default)
[–]**stwrap**	disable/[enable] line shortening
susp *c*	use *c* to suspend all foreground processes (^Z default)
swtch *c*	exit to **shl** command from layer (^Z default)
tab*n*	set output delay after horizontal tab (**0** to **3**)
[–]**tabs**	[expand to spaces]/preserve output tabs
term	set all modes for the specified terminal, *term* (**tty33**, **tty37**, **vt05**, **tn300**, **ti700**, and **tek** allowed)
time *c*	set **TIME** value to *c* (used with **– icanon**)
[–]**tostop**	[do not] send SIGTTOU when background process writes to terminal
tsetcoff	xmit clock not provided
tsetcrbrg	output rec baud rate generator on EIA-232-D pin 24
tsetctbrg	output xmit baud rate generator on EIA-232-D pin 24
tsetcrset	output RC on EIA-232-D pin 24
tsetctset	output TC on EIA-232-D pin 24
vt*n*	set output delay after vertical tab (**0** or **1**)
werase *c*	use *c* to erase preceding "word"
[–]**xcase**	[do not] change case on local output
xpixels *n*	set horizontal window size to *n* pixels
xcibrg	use internal baud generator for xmit clock
xcrset	use EIA-232-D pin 17 as xmit clock
xctset	use EIA-232-D pin 15 as xmit clock
ypixels *n*	set vertical window size to *n* pixels

Note: there may be additional video modes associated with a particular console device

β **STTY** — Set Terminal Options
% **stty** [*roptions*] [*options*]
% **STTY** [*roptions*] [*options*]
Roptions (reporting options):

– a	print all option settings
– g	print settings in **stty** argument format
– h	print settings in with control characters in columnar format
all	like default but control characters in columnar format
everything	
	same as **–h** format
speed	report only terminal speed
size	show window size in rows and columns

Options (set options):

0	hang up phone line
async	set normal async mode with clock modes **xcibrg**, **rcibrg**, **tsetcoff** and **rsetcoff**
brk *c*	set break character to *c*

(continued)

[–]**brkint**	[do not] send **INTR** signal on input break
bsn	set output delay after backspace (**0** or **1**)
[–]**cbreak**	same as **–icanon**/[**canon**]
[–]**clocal**	[enable]/disable modem control
cols n	same as **columns** c
columns n	
	set window to n columns
cooked	disable raw input & output
	(same as **– raw**)
[–]**cread**	[disable]/enable receiver
crn	set output delay after carriage return (**0-3**)
crt	set **echoe**, **echoctl** and, if speed >= 1200,
	echoke
crterase	same as **echoe**
crtkill	same as **echoke**
[–]**crtscts**	enable RTS/CTS flow control σ
csn	set character size to n bits (**5** to **8**)
[–]**cstopb**	set [one]/two stop bits per character
ctab c	set CTAB char to c (used with **–stappl**)
[–]**ctlecho**	same as [–]**echoctl**
[–]**ctsxon**	[disable]/enable CTS output flow control
dec	set erase to DEL, kill to ˆU, intr to ˆC,
	set **decctlq** and **crt**
[–]**decctlq**	same as [**ixany**]/**–ixany**
[–]**dterxoff**	
	[disable]/enable DTER (EIA-232-D pin 20)
	input flow control
dsusp c	use c to suspend process on next read
[–]**echo**	[do not] echo all input characters
[–]**echoctl**	[do not] echo control chars as ˆ*char*
[–]**echoe**	[do not] echo **ERASE** for CRTs
[–]**echok**	[do not] echo a newline after **KILL**
[–]**echoke**	[do not] BS-SP-BS erase line on line kill
[–]**echonl**	[do not] echo newlines
[–]**echoprt**	[do not] echo erase char as char is
	"erased"
ek	reset **ERASE** to # and **KILL** to @
eof c	set end of file character to c
eol c	set additional line delimiter to c
eol2 c	set another line delimiter to c
erase c	set character **ERASE** character to c
[–]**even**	same as [–]/**evenp**
[–]**evenp**	same as [–]**parenb** and **cs**[**8**]/**7**
ffn	set output delay after form-feed (**0** or **1**)
flush c	set flush character to c
[–]**flusho**	[do not]/flush output buffers
[–]**hup**	[do not]/do hang up on last close
[–]**hupcl**	same as **hup**
[–]**icanon**	[disable]/enable checking for
	ERASE and **KILL**
[–]**icrnl**	[do not] map CR to NL on input
[–]**iexten**	[disable]/enable extended input functions
[–]**ignbrk**	[do not] ignore break on input
[–]**igncr**	[do not] ignore CR on input
[–]**ignpar**	[do not] ignore parity errors

(continued)

STTY, continued

[–]**imaxbel**	[do not] echo BEL when input too long
[–]**inlcr**	[do not] map input newline to carriage return
[–]**inpck**	[disable]/enable input parity check
intr *c*	set **INTR** (interrupt) character to *c*
[–]**isig**	[disable]/enable checking for **INTR**, **SWTCH** and **QUIT**
ispeed *n*	set input baud rate to *n* (**0** indicates **ispeed** is to be set to **ospeed**)
[–]**istrip**	[do not] strip 8th bit of input characters
[–]**isxoff**	[disable]/enable isochronous input flow control
[–]**iuclc**	[do not] map input upper case to lower
[–]**ixany**	allow [**START**]/any character to restart **STOP**
[–]**ixoff**	[disable]/enable **XSTART/STOP** during input
[–]**ixon**	[disable]/enable **START/STOP** protocol
kill *c*	set line **KILL** character to *c*
[–]**lcase**	same as [–]**xcase**, [–]**iuclc**, and [–]**olcuc**
[–]**LCASE**	same as [–]**lcase**
[–]**line** *n*	set line discipline to *n* (**1** to **126** allowed)
[–]**litout**	[enable]/disable **parenb**, **istrip**, **opost** and set [**cs7**]/**cs8**
lnext *c*	use *c* to escape special meaning of next char
[–]**loblk**	[do not] block output from non-current layer
[–]**markp**	[disable]/enable **parenb**, **parodd**, **parext**, **cs7**/[**cs8**]
min *c*	set **MIN** value to *c* (used with – **icanon**) **parodd** and **parext**
n	set terminal baud rate to *n*
[–]**nl**	same as [**icrnl**]/– **icrnl** and [**onlcr**]/– **onlcr** [and – **inlcr**, – **igncr**, – **ocrnl**, and – **onlret**]
nl*n*	set output delay after newline (**0** or **1**)
[–]**noflsh**	[do not] no flush after **INTR** or **QUIT** or **SWTCH**
[–]**ocrnl**	[do not] map output carriage return to newline
[–]**odd**	same as [–]**oddp**
[–]**oddp**	same as [–]**parenb**, [–]**parodd**, and **cs**[**8**]/**7**
[–]**ofdel**	set fill character to [**NUL**]/**DEL**
[–]**ofill**	delay output with [timing]/fill characters
[–]**olcuc**	[do not] map output lower case to upper case
[–]**onlcr**	[do not] map output newline to carriage return
[–]**onlret**	terminal does [not] carriage return after newline
[–]**onocr**	[do not] output carriage return at column 0
[–]**opost**	[do not] post-process output

(continued)

ospeed *n*	set output baud rate to *n* (**0** causes an immediate hangup)
[−]**parenb**	[disable]/enable parity detection and generation
[−]**parext**	[disable]/enable checking for mark and space parity
[−]**parity**	same as [−]**parenb** and **cs**[**8**]/**7**
[−]**parmrk**	[do not] mark parity errors
[−]**parodd**	select [even]/odd parity
[−]**pass8**	[enable]/disable **parenb** and **istrip**; set [**cs7**]/**cs8**
[−]**pendin**	[do not] retype pending input at next read
[−]**prterase**	same as [−]**echoprt**
quit *c*	set **QUIT** character to *c*
[−]**raw**	[disable]/enable raw input and output
rcibrg	use internal baud generator for rec clock
rcrset	use EIA-232-D pin 17 as xmit clock
rctset	use EIA-232-D pin 15 as xmit clock
[−]**rlsdxon**	[disable]/enable RLSD (EIA-232-D pin 8) output flow control
rprnt *c*	*c* will cause all unread characters to be reprinted
rows *n*	set window size to *n* rows
rsetcoff	rec clock not provided
rsetcrc	output RC on CCITT V.24, ckt. 128
rsetcxc	output TC on CCITT V.24, ckt. 128
[−]**rtsxoff**	[disable]/enable RTS input flow control
sane	reset all modes to "sane" values
[−]**spacep**	[disable]/enable **parenb**, **cs7** and **parext**
[−]**stappl**	use application/[line] mode on sync. line
start *c*	use *c* to resume output
[−]**stflush**	enable/[disable] **flush** after **write**
stop *c*	use *c* to suspend output
[−]**stwrap**	disable/[enable] line shortening
susp *c*	use *c* to suspend all foreground processes
swtch *c*	exit to **shl** command from layer
tab*n*	set output delay after horizontal tab (**0-3**)
[−]**tabs**	[expand to spaces]/preserve output tabs
[−]**tandem**	same as ixoff
term	set all modes for the specified terminal, *term*; (**tty33**, **tty37**, **vt05**, **tn300**, **ti700**, and **tek** allowed)
time *c*	set **TIME** value to *c* (used with −**icanon**)
[−]**tostop**	[do not] send SIGTTOU when background process writes to terminal
tsetcoff	xmit clock not provided
tsetcrc	output RC on EIA-232-D pin 24
tsetcxc	output TC on EIA-232-D pin 24
vt*n*	set output delay after vertical tab (**0** or **1**)
werase *c*	use *c* to erase preceding "word"
[−]**xcase**	[do not] change case on local output
xcibrg	use internal baud generator for xmit clock
xcrset	use EIA-232-D pin 17 as xmit clock
xctset	use EIA-232-D pin 15 as xmit clock
xpixels *n*	set horizontal window size to *n* pixels

(continued)

STTY, continued
    ypixels *n* set vertical window size to *n* pixels

SU — Become Another User
% **su** [*option*] [*user* [*args*]]
Option:
    –   change environment as if user logged in

SUM — Compute File Checksum
% **sum** [*option*] *file*
Option:
    – r   use alternate checksum algorithm

β **SUM** — Compute File Checksum
% **/usr/ucb/sum** *file*

$\xi\kappa\sigma$ **SUSPEND** — Halt Current Shell
% **suspend**

SVR4.MAKE — System V Make
% **/usr/ccs/lib/svr4.make** [*options*] [*names*]
see **MAKE**
Note: if env variable **USE_SVR4_MAKE** is set, **make**
will invoke this version.

ξ **SWITCH** — Structured Conditional
% **switch** (*expr*)
    case *cmp***:**
                  cmds
                  breaksw

    ...

    default:
                  cmds
  endsw

expr	a valid C shell expression (not regex)
cmp,...	comparison to *expr* result
cmds	a valid Solaris or C shell command

SYMORDER — Reorder Symbol List
% **symorder** [*option*] *ojbfile symbolfile*
Options:
    – s   silent

objfile	file whose symbols are to be rearranged
symbolfile	list of symbols to be replaced at head of list

SYNC — Write Unwritten Info in Memory to Disk
% **sync**

TABS — Set Terminal Tabs
% **tabs** [*taboption*] [**– T***type*] [**+m***n*]
taboption: set tabs at columns; only use 1 option

– – *file*	first line of *file* read for tab specifier
– 8	standard tabs, every 8 columns (default)
– a	1,10,16,36,72 (Assembler, IBM S/370)
– a2	1,10,16,40,72 (Assembler, IBM S/370)

(continued)

TABS, continued

– c	1,8,12,16,20,55 (normal COBOL)
– c2	1,6,10,14,49 (compact COBOL)
– c3	1,6,10,14,18,22,26,30,34,38,42,46,50,54, 58,62,67 (COBOL)
– f	1,7,11,15,19,23 (FORTRAN)
– *n*	1*n, 2*n, ...
n1,n2,...	arbitrary ascending values (up to 40 in list) if a number is preceded by + it is added
– p	1,5,9,13,17,21,25,29,33,37,41,45,49,53, 57,61
– s	1,10,55 (SNOBOL)
– u	1,12,20,44 (UNIVAC 1100 Assembler)
+ m*n*	left margin, added to tab stops (**10** default)
– T*type*	terminal type (**$TERM** default)

TAIL — Output Last Part of File
% **/usr/bin/tail** [*options*] [*file*]
% **/usr/xpg4/bin/tail** [*options*] [**-c** *n*] [*file*]
% **/usr/xpg4/bin/tail** [*options*] [**-n** *n*] [*file*]
    stdin read if *file* not specified
Options:

– c*n*	copying starts relative to the beginning (+*n*) or end (-*n* or *n* with no sign) of the file
– f	follow growth of *file* (don't stop at end of file)
+*n* [**bcl**]	begin *n* units from beginning of *file*, may be **b**locks, **c**haracters, or **l**ines (default)
– [*n*] [**bcl**]	begin *n* units before end of *file* (**10** default)
– r	reverse order (can't use with **-f**, **b**, **c**, **l**)

TALK — Talk to Another User
% **talk** *user* [*tty*]

Control-L will redraw the screen
exit with interrupt character

TAR — Tape File Archiver
% **/usr/sbin/tar** – [*key*] [*files*]
    stdin read if no *files* specified
Key Format: *letter* [*modifier*]
Key Letters:

c	create new tape and record *files*, implies **r**
r	record *files* onto end of tape
t	tell when *files* found, all entries if no *files*
u	update tapes by adding *files* if not on tape or if modified since being last written to tape
x	extract *files*, entire tape if no *files*

Key Modifiers:

b *n*	*n* is blocking factor (**1** default, **20** max)
B	force extra reads to fill block

(continued)

TAR, continued

f *arch*	*arch* is the file to be used for input/output to archives (if – then **stdin** read or **stdout** written
e	quit on minor error
F	exclude RCS/SCCS directories
FF	exclude RCS/SCCS directories, .o, errs, core, and a.out files
h	follow symbolic links
i	ignore checksum errors on archive
l	complain if all file links not found
m	update file modification times to time on file in archive
n	**archive**=*n* entry of **/etc/default/tar** describes device (TAPE environment variable or " " default)
o	set user and group ID of extracted files to user running **tar**
p	ignore umask value in restoring permissions
v	verbose mode
w	wait for confirmation after reporting filename (**y** causes action to be performed)
X *xfile*	exclude files named in *xfile* from archive

TBL — Table Formatter for **troff**

% **tbl** [*options*] [*files*]

   stdin read if no *files* specified

Options:

– me	include **me** macro package
– mm	include **mm** macro package
– ms	include **ms** macro package

TCOPY — Copy Magnetic Tape

% **tcopy** *source* [*destination*]

if only *source* is specified, the tape is read and statistics are printed only

TEE — Copy **stdin** to **stdout** and Files

% **tee** [*options*] [*files*]

Options:

– a	append to *files* instead of overwriting
– i	ignore interrupts

TELNET — Connect to Remote Using TELNET Protocol

% **telnet** [*options*] [*host* [*port*]]

Options:

– 8	8 bit data path
– c	don't read **.telnetrc** in the user's home directory
– d	set initial **debug** toggle to true
– e *esc*	set initial escape character to *esc*
– E	prevent any character from being seen as an escape
– l *user*	*user* as login name (if **ENVIRON** option understood on remote)

(continued)

TELNET, continued

– L	8 bit data path on output
– n *file*	open *file* for recording trace information
– r	rlogin like interface

Commands:

? [*cmd*] help with *cmd*
    if no *cmd*, prints help summary

close close all open TELNET sessions and exit

display [*args*]
    display specified **set** and **toggle** values
    (all values default)

environ *arguments*
    manipulate variables that may be sent
    through TELNET ENVIRON option
    Valid arguments are:
    ? print help for **environ**
    define *var val*
        define a variable and its value
    export*var*
        mark *var* to be exported to
        theremote side
    list list the current set of environment
        variables
    undefine *var*
        undefine a variable
    unexport*var*
        unexport *var*

logout *type* sends **telnet logout** option
    to the remote side (if supported)

mode *type* go to specified mode if available
    ? print help for **mode**
    character
        character at a time mode
    [–] **edit** try to enable EDIT mode of
        LINEMODE option
    line line mode
    [–] **isig** try to enable TRAPSIG mode of
        LINEMODE option
    [–] **litecho**
        try to enable LIT_ECHO mode of
        LINEMODE option
    [–] **softtabs**
        try to enable SOFT_TAB mode of
        LINEMODE option

open [–l *user*] *host* [*port*]
    open connection to host

quit same as **close**

send *args* send special character sequences
    to remote
    ? print help menu for **send**
    abort abort process
    ao abort output
    ayt are you there?
    brk break
    do *op* do protocol option negotiation
        (debugging)

(continued)

           dont *op* don't do protocol option
                      negotiation (debugging)

ec	erase character
el	erase line
eof	end of file
eor	end of record
escape	escape
ga	go ahead
getstatus	
	get option status
ip	interrupt process
nop	no operation
susp	suspend process
synch	SYNCH (discard unread input)
will *op*	will do protocol option negotiation (debugging)
wont *op*	wont do protocol option negotiation (debugging)

set *var value*

	specify value for variable
?	display legal set and unset commands
ayt	are you there?
echo	toggle local echo (ˆ**E** default)
eof	end-of-file character for remote
erase	erase character
escape	escape character (ˆ] default)
flushoutput	
	abort output
forwn	forward partial lines (*n* is 1 or 2)
interrupt	
	interrupt process
kill	erase line
lnext	telnet lnext character assumed to be that of terminal in old line by line mode
quit	break
reprint	telnet reprint character assumed to be that of terminal in old line by line mode
rlogin	rlogin escape character assumed
start	telnet **start** character assumed
stop	telnet **stop** character assumed
susp	use TELNET SUSP suspend sequence
tracefile	
	file to which **netdata** or **debug** output is sent
worderase	
	telnet **worderase** taken to be that of terminal

slc *state* (Set Local Characters)

	specify *state* for special characters
?	help information on **slc**
check	verifies settings for current

(continued)

TELNET, continued

	export	switches to local defaults
	import	switches to remote defaults
status	show status	
toggle *args*		

       toggle flags

       ?   display local **toggle** commands

       autoflush
           interrupt or quit sent to remote
           (stty value default)

       autosynch
           synch after **interrupt** or **quit**
           (off default)

       binary   endable/disable telnet binary
           option on both input and output

       crlf   <cr><lf> if TRUE, <cr><null> if
           FALSE (default)

       crmod   map output <cr> to <cr><lf>
           (no map default)

       debug   toggle socket level debugging
           (off default)

       localchars
           when on, recognizes local
           commands which are transformed
           to remote control sequences
           (on in line, off in char
           mode default)

       inbinary
           enable/disable telnet binary
           option on input

       netdata
           toggle display of network data in
           hex (off default)

       options
           toggle display of internal protocol
           processing (off default)

       outbinary
           enable/disable telnet binary
           option on output

       prettydump
           out from **netdata** is more readable

       skiprc   when TRUE, skip reading of
           .telnetrc file in user's home
           directory

       termdata
           toggle display of all terminal data
           in hexadecimal format

  unset *var*

       See **set** options

  z   suspend **telnet**. Only works in shell
       with job control

host   host name or Internet address in dot notation

port   port number (uses default if not specified)

β **TEST** — Test Conditions
% **test** [*cond*]
% [*cond*]

cond   valid condition in the shell; can be built
as below (except no – **h**) with the
additional condition:
     – **L** *file*   returns true if file is symbolic link
         and exists

TEST — Test Conditions
% **test** *cond*
% [*cond*]
cond   valid condition in the shell
Conditions:

– **b** *file*	true if *file* exists and is a block special file
– **c** *file*	true if *file* exists and is a character special file
– **d** *file*	true if *file* exists and is a directory
– **f** *file*	true if *file* exists and is a regular file
– **g** *file*	true if *file* exists and has set-**GID** bit set
– **h** *file*	true if *file* exists and is a symbolic link
– **k** *file*	true if *file* exists and has sticky bit set
– **L** *file*	true if *file* exists and is a symbolic link
– **n** *string*	true if *string* is of non-zero length
n1 – **eq** *n2*	true if integers *n1* and *n2* equal
n1 – **ge** *n2*	true if integer *n1* ≥ and *n2*
n1 – **gt** *n2*	true if integer *n1* > *n2*
n1 – **le** *n2*	true if integer *n1* ≤ *n2*
n1 – **lt** *n2*	true if integer *n1* < *n2*
n1 – **ne** *n2*	true if integers *n1* and *n2* unequal
– **p** *file*	true if *file* exists and is a named pipe
– **r** *file*	true if *file* exists and is readable
– **s** *file*	true if *file* exists and has a non-zero size
string	true if *string* is not the null string
s1 = *s2*	true if strings *s1* and *s2* are the same
s1 != *s2*	true if strings *s1* and *s2* are not the same
– **t** [*fd*]	true if descriptor *fd* associated with a terminal
– **u** *file*	true if *file* exists and has set-**UID** bit set
– **w** *file*	true if *file* exists and is writable
– **x** *file*	true if *file* exists and is executable
– **z** *string*	true if *string* has zero length

Expressions may be joined by

!	logical negation
– **a**	logical and
– **o**	logical or
(*cond*)	parentheses for grouping must be quoted to prevent misinterpretation by shell

TFTP — Trivial File Transfer Program
% **tftp** [*host*]

TIME — Print a Command's Elapsed, System and
　　User Times
% **time** [**-p**] *cmd*
Options:
　　– p　　　　　write timing output to **stderr** in
　　the following format:
　　real %f\nuser %f\nsys %f\n *<real scnds>*,
　　　　　　　<user scnds>, *<system scnds>*

κσ **TIMES** — Report Time Usages of Current Shell
% **times**

TIMEX — Print a Command's Time and System Activity
% **timex** [*options*] *cmd*
Options:
　　– o　　　　　report number of blocks read and
　　　　　　　written and total characters transferred
　　– p[*opt*]　report process activity for *cmd*
　　　　　　　and its children
　　　　f　　　print fork/exec flag & exit status
　　　　h　　　print CPU time/elapsed time
　　　　k　　　print kcore-minutes
　　　　m　　　print mean core size
　　　　r　　　print user time/(sys+user time)
　　　　t　　　separate user and system CPU
　　　　　　　times
　　– s　　　　　report all system activity during
　　　　　　　cmd execution

TIP — Connect to Remote System
% **tip** [*options*] *host*
Options:
　　– v　　　　　display **.tiprc** lines as executed
　　– *speed*　　set baud rate to *speed*
　　　　　　　(**tip0** entry default)
host　　　　　machine name or phone number

enter **~?** when in **tip** for tilde command summary

TNFDUMP — Convert TNF file to ASCII
% **tnfdump** [**-r**] *tnf-file*
Options:
　　– r　　　　　do raw conversion of TNF to ASCII

TNFXTRACT — Extract Kernel Probes Output
　　into a Trace File
% **tnfdump** [**-d** *dumpfile* **-n** *namelist*] *tnf-file*
Options:
　　– d *dumpfile*
　　　　　　　use *dumpfile* as the system
　　　　　　　memory image
　　– n *namelist*
　　　　　　　use *namelist* as the file containing
　　　　　　　symbol table information for *dumpfile*

TOUCH — Update File Access/Modification Times
% **touch** [*options*] *files*
Options:

– a	update only access time
– c	do not create non-existent *files*
– m	update only modification time
– r *ref_file*	use times of file named by *ref_file*
– t *time*	use the specified *time*
MMDDhhmm [*yy*]	
	new time (current time default)

β **TOUCH** — Update File Access/Modification Times
% **touch** [*options*] *files*
Options:

– c	do not create non-existent *files*
– f	attempt to force touch despite any protections

TPLOT — Graphics Filter(s) for Plotters
% **/usr/bin/tplot** [-**T** *terminal*]
See also **plot**

TPUT — Find Out Terminal-Dependent Capabilities
% **tput** [*option*] *arg*
% **tput – S** [*option*]
    reads *args* from **stdin**
Option:

– S <<	allows more than one capability per invocation
– T*type*	specify terminal type (**$TERM** default)

Arguments:

cap [*parameters*]	
	output sequence associated with *cap*
cap	name of capability in **terminfo** database
parameters	parameters passed to *cap*

Common Capabilities:

blink	turn on blinking
bold	turn on extra-bright mode
civis	make cursor invisible
clear	clear screen & home cursor
cnorm	make cursor normal
cols	outputs number of columns on screen
cub1	move cursor left 1 space
cud1	move cursor down 1 line
cup *r c*	move cursor to row *r*, column *c*
cuu1	move cursor up 1 line
cvvis	make cursor very visible
dim	turn on half-bright mode
flash	visible bell
hc	hard copy terminal
home	move cursor to home
init	output terminal initialization string
invis	turn on invisible text mode
lines	outputs number of lines on screen

(continued)

TPUT, continued

longname	print long name of terminal type
reset	output the terminal's reset string
rev	turn on reverse video
rmso	end standout mode
rmul	end underscore mode
smso	start standout mode
smul	start underscore mode

TR — Translate Characters

% **/usr/bin/tr** [*options*] [*string1*] [*string2*]
% **/usr/xpg4/bin/tr** [*options*] [*string1*] [*string2*]
Options:

– c	use characters not in *string1* in place of *string1*
– d	delete characters in *string1* from input
– s	squeeze repeated output characters in *string2*

Strings may include:

[*a – z*]	short form for range of characters from *a* to *z*
[*a*n*]	short form for *n* repetitions of character *a*
n	ASCII character whose octal value is *n* (1 to 3 digits)

Note: You need to type the brackets around the strings

β TR — Translate Characters

% **/usr/ucb/tr** [*options*] [*string1* [*string2*]]

– c	use characters not in *string1* in place of *string1*
– d	delete characters in *string1* from input
– s	squeeze repeated output characters in *string2*

Strings may include:

a – z	short form for range of characters from *a* to *z*
a*n	short form for *n* repetitions of character *a*
n	ASCII character whose octal value is *n* (1 to 3 digits)

κσ TRAP — Trap Hardware Signals

See **Built-in Commands** in the Solaris SHELL section
Pages 168-172

TROFF — Typeset Documents

% **troff** [*options*] [*files*]
 stdin read if no *files* specified
Options:

– a	output ASCII approximation to **stdout**
– f	don't print trailer page
– F*dir*	search *dir* for font tables
– i	read **stdin** after all files

(continued)

TROFF, continued

–m_name_	prepend macro file **/usr/ucblib/doctools/tmac.**_name_
–n_n_	number first page _n_
–o_list_	print only listed page numbers
–q	quiet mode in **nroff**; ignored in **nroff**
–r_an_	set number register _a_ to _n_ (_a_ is one character only)
–s[_n_]	stop every n pages (**1** default)
–T_name_	specify output device type
–u[_n_]	set emboldening on position 3 to _n_ (**0** default)
–z	suppress formatted output (diagnostics only)
list	comma-separated, _n–m_ is range, _–n_ in beginning to page _n_, _n–_ is page _n_ to end

TRUE — Return Successful Exit Status
% **true**

TRUSS — Trace System Calls and Signals
% **truss** [_options_] _cmd_
Options:

–a	show arguments to each **exec()**
–c	only count calls, faults and signals instead of line by line trace
–e	show environment strings passed to **exec()**
–f	follow all children created by **fork()**
–i	don't display interruptible sleeping calls
–l	include ID of responsible lightweight process
–m[!]_fault_	machine faults to trace or exclude (**–mall –m!fltpage** default)
–o _ofile_	write output to _ofile_ (**stderr** default)
–p	interpret _cmd_ as list of process IDs
–r[!]_fd_	show buffer contents for reads on specified file descriptors (**–r!all** default)
–s[!]_signal_	signals to trace or exclude (**–sall** default)
–t[!]_call_	system calls to trace or exclude (**–tall** default)
–v[!]_call_	show structures on system calls (**–v!all** default)
–w[!]_fd_	show buffer contents for writes on specified file descriptors (**–w!all** default)
–x[!]_call_	show call arguments in raw form (**–x!all** default)

Notes:	**!** is used to negate the meaning of an option **all** can be used to specify all members of a list. All lists are comma-delimited
cmd	UNIX command to execute or pid list with **–p** option

TSET — Establish Terminal Characteristics
% **tset** [*options*] [*type*]
Options:

–	output terminal type to **stdout**
– e[*c*]	set erase character to *c* (BACKSPACE default)
– E[*c*]	like **– e** except only for terminals that can BACKSPACE
– I	suppress transmitting init strings
– k[*c*]	set kill character to *c* (^U default)
– m[*port*[*baud*]:*type*]	
	map *port* and *baud* rate to a specific terminal *type*
– n	new tty driver modes are initialized
– Q	suppress "set to" messages
– r	output terminal type to **stderr**
– s	output **setenv** or **export** commands
– S	output environment strings only

type is terminal type as in **termcap** file

TSORT — Topological Sort
% **/usr/ccs/bin/tsort** [*file*]
    stdin read if no *file* specified

TTY — Display Terminal's Name
% **tty** [*option*]
Options:

– l	print synchronous line number if connected
– s	silent mode, no output: successful exit status if **stdin** is a terminal

Exit Codes:

0	**stdin** is a terminal
1	**stdin** is not a terminal
2	invalid option specified

TYPE — Describe Command Type
% **type** [*cmd*]

TYPESET — Set Shell Environment Values
% **typeset** [+I -I\f(Sioptions] [*defs*]
Options:

– f	names refer to functions
– H	set Unix host-name file mapping on non-Unix machine
– i	parameter is an integer
– l	lowercase all
– L	left justify and remove leading blanks from *val* that can BACKSPACE
– r	readonly
– R	right justify and fill with leading blanks
– t	tag variables
– u	uppercase all
– x	export definitions

(continued)

TYPESET, continued
    −Z   right justify and fill with leading zeros

defs   definitions of the form *name*[=*val*]

UL — Underline
% **ul** [*options*] [*files*]
    stdin read if no *files* specified
Options:
    −i   underline on separate line
                 result to **stdout**
    −t [*term*] override terminal type with *term*

ULIMIT — Set Resources Available to Shell and Descendents
% **/usr/bin/ulimit** [-**f**] [*512-byte-block-maximum*]

ξ ULIMIT — Set Resources Available to Shell and Descendents
% **ulimit** [-**h**] [*resource*]
Option:
    −h   use hard limits

$\kappa\,\sigma$ ULIMIT — Set Resources Available to Shell and Descendents
% **ulimit** [*options*] [*limit*]
Options:
    −a   print all limits
    −c   max core size (in 512-byte blocks)
    −d   max size of data segment or heap (in kbytes)
    −f   max file size (in 512-byte blocks)
    −H   use hard limits
    −n   max file descriptor plus 1
    −s   max size of stack segment (in kbytes)
    −S   use soft limits
    −t   max CPU time in seconds
    −v   max size of virtual memory (in kbytes)

UMASK — Set File Creation Mask Utility
% **umask** [-**S**] [*ugo*]
    current mask printed if no arguments specified
Option:
    -**S**   produce symbolic output

ugo   3 digit octal code specifying denied file access permissions. Each of the *ugo* digits formed of *read* (04), *write* (02), & *execute* (01) permissions for the classifications of *u*ser, *g*roup, & *o*thers.

κ UMASK — Set File Creation Mask
% **umask** [-**S**] [*ugo*]
KornShell umask arguments same as **umask** general utility

ξσ UMASK — Set File Creation Mask
% **umask** [*ugo*]
Shell umask *ugo* argument same as **umask** general utility

UNALIAS — Remove Pseudonym(s)
% **/usr/bin/unalias** [**- a**] [*names*]

names   one or more alias names
Option:
     – a   Remove all aliases

ξ UNALIAS — Remove Pseudonym(s)
% **/usr/bin/unalias** [*pattern*]

pattern   pattern to match aliases to remove

κ UNALIAS — Remove Pseudonym(s)
% **/usr/bin/unalias** [*names*]

names   one or more alias names to remove

UNAME — Print System Name
% **uname** [*options*]
Options:
     – a   print all information
     – i   print platform name
     – m   print hardware name
     – n   print node name
     – p   print host's processor type
     – r   print operating system release
     – s   print operating system name (default)
     – v   print version number of operating system

UNCOMPRESS — Uncompress File
% **uncompress** [**-cvf**] *file*
(See **compress** for a description of options)

UNEXPAND — Replace Spaces with Tabs
% **unexpand** [*option*] [*files*]
stdin read if no *files* specified
Options:
     – a   convert all sequences of two or more
                      SPACE characters to TABs
                      (only leading TABs default)

UNGET — Void SCCS File Get
% **unget** [*options*] *files*
     names of SCCS files read from **stdin** if *files* is –
Options:
     – n   do not remove file retrieved with **get**
     – r*sid*   specify SCCS ID of version to void
     – s   suppress output of SCCS ID on **stdout**

ξ UNHASH — Disable Internal Hash Table
% **unhash**

UNIFDEF — Resolve and Remove C **ifdef**ed Lines
% **unifdef** [*options*] [*file*]
Options: (one or more of **D**, **U**, **iD**, or **iU** required)

– **c**	complement of normal output
– **D**[*name*]	lines associated with defined symbol *name*
– **iD**[*name*]	print out but don't process lines associated with defined symbol *name*
– **iU**[*name*]	print out but don't process lines associated with undefined symbol *name*
– **l**	replace removed lines with blank lines
– **t**	don't attempt to recognize comments and quotes
– **U**[*name*]	ignore lines associated with undefined symbol *name*

UNIQ — Report Repeated Lines
% **uniq** [*options*] [*input* [*output*]]
    stdin read if *input* and *output* not specified
    stdout written if *output* not specified
Options:

– **c**	output unique lines, count repeated ones
– **d**	only one copy of repeated lines output
– **f** *flds*	ignore first *flds* fields on each input line when doing comparisons
– *n*	skip *n* fields from start of line
+*n*	skip *n* characters from start of field
– **s** *chars*	ignore first *chars* characters when doing comparisons
– **u**	only unique lines in *input* output (default also outputs one occurrence of repeated lines)

UNITS — Interactive Measurement Units Conversion
% **units**

UNIX2DOS — Convert Text Files to DOS Format
% **unix2dos** [*option*] [*infile* [*outfile*]]
stdin read if *infile* not specified
stdout written if *outfile* not specified
Options:

– **7**	convert 8-bit characters to DOS 7-bit
– **ascii**	add returns
– **iso**	convert ISO characters to DOS extended character set (default)

if *outfile* not specified, *infile* is overwritten

UNPACK — Unpack Compressed File (See **PACK**)
% **unpack** *files*.**z**
    unpack from *files*.**z** to *files*

ξ **UNSET** — Remove Variables
% **unset** *pattern*

ϕ **UNSET** — Unset Environment Variable
% **unset** [*options*] *vars*
Options:
    – f*file*   unsets variable in global
                    environment; *file* contains lines of form
                    var=val
    – l   unsets variable in local environment

κ **UNSET** — Remove Variables
% **unset – f** *name*
Options:
    – f   disables file name generation

σ **UNSET** — Remove Variables
% **unset** *name*

ξ **UNSET** — Remove An Environment Variable
% **unset** *var*

$\kappa\sigma$ **UNTIL** — Conditional Looping Command
See **Control Commands** in the Solaris SHELL section
Pages 168-172

UPTIME — Display System Uptime
% **uptime**

β **USERS** — Display List of Logged In Users
% **/usr/ucb/users** [*file*]
file where to find information (**/var/adm/utmp** default)

UUCP — UNIX to UNIX Copy
% **uucp** [*options*] *files dest*
Options:
    – c   use *files* directly when transferring
                    (default)
    – C   copy *files* to spool directory
                    before transmit
    – d   make all required directories (default)
    – f   do not make intermediate directories
    – g*grade*   set job priority
    – j   print job ID on **stdout**
    – m   send mail to requester when complete
    – n*user*   notify *user* on remote system
                    when *file* sent
    – r   queue files but don't initiate transfer
    – s*file*   report status to *file*, must
                    be full pathname
    – x*level*   debugging at *level*

    dest   destination consists of
                    [*sys_name*!]*pathname*
                    ˜ may be used to specify user's directory
    grade   letter or number; lower ASCII sequence
                    gives higher priority
    level   0–9; higher numbers give more
                    information

UUDECODE — Decode ASCII Representation of File
% **uudecode** [**- p**] [*encoded_file*]
    stdin read if no files specified

encoded-file is decoded and resulting file is written
to name specified in *encoded-file*
Options:
    – p   decode *encoded_file* and send it to **stdout**

UUENCODE — Encode Binary File into ASCII
% **uuencode** [*source_file*] *file_label*

source_file   name of file to encode
            stdin read if file not specified
file_label   file name to use when decoding

UUGLIST — Print Service Grade List
% **uuglist** [*option*]
Option:
    – u   print grades allowed by user

UULOG — **uucp** Log Maintainer (See **UUCP**)
% **uulog** [*options*] [*sys*]
Options:
    – f*sys*   **tail – f** of file transfer log for system *sys*
    – n   **tail –** *n* of log
    – s*sys*   print information on work with system *sys*
    – x   look in **uuxqt** log file for system

sys is system name; can be specified in either place

UUNAME — List **uucp** Names of Systems (See **UUCP**)
% **uuname** [*options*]
Options:
    – c   print **cu** names of systems
    – l   print local system name

UUPICK — Accept/Reject **uuto** Files (See **UUTO**)
% **uupick** [*option*]
Option:
    – s*sys*   only search PUBDIR for files from
             system *sys*

UUSTAT — **uucp** Status and Job Control
% **uustat** [*options*]
General Status/Cancel Options:
    – a   output all jobs in queue
    – j   list total number of jobs displayed
    – k*id*   kill **uucp** job identifier *id*
    – m   report accessibility status for all systems
    – n   suppress **stdout**, show **stderr**
    – p   execute **ps – flp** for all PIDs in lock files
    – q   report job numbers, control files
             & time oldest & youngest files queued
             for each system
    – r*n*   set last modified time of job *n* to current
             time

(continued)

Remote Performance Options:

−c	display average queue time, not average transfer rate
−d_n_	use _n_ minutes in calculations (**60** default)
−t_sys_	report transfer rate or queue time for _sys_

Remote System/User Status Options:

−s_sys_	status of requests logged with _sys_
−S_flgs_	report job state
	flgs are:
	c completed
	i interrupted
	q queued
	r running
−u_user_	status of requests from _user_

all options except **−s** and **−u** are mutually exclusive

UUTO — Public UNIX-to-UNIX File Copy
% **uuto** [_options_] _files dest_
Options:

−m	mail when copy is completed
−p	copy _files_ to spool directory before transmit

UUX — Remote UNIX Command Execution
% **uux** [_option_] _cmd_
Option:

−	**uux**'s **stdin** becomes _cmd_'s **stdin**
−a_user_	user ID is _user_ (user running **uux** default)
−b	return input if exit status is non-zero
−c	don't copy file to spool directory (default)
−C	file to spool directory
−g_grade_	set job priority
−j	print job ID
−n	don't notify user
−p	same as **−**
−r	queue files but don't initiate transfer
−s_file_	report status to _file_, must be full pathname
−x_level_	debugging at _level_
−z	notify user if successful
grade	letter or number; lower ASCII sequence gives higher priority
level	0−9; higher numbers give more information

VACATION — Automatically Respond to Mail
% **vacation -I**
    start **/usr/ucb/vacation**;
    return **stdin** message with ˜**/.vacation.msg**
    to sender; log message in ˜**/.vacation.pag** and
    ˜**/.vacation.dir**
% **vacation** [*options*]
    interactively turn **vacation** on or off
Options:

– a*alias user*	make *alias* valid for *user* so mail addressed to *alias* gets reply
– j	don't check whether recipient is in **To:** or **cc:** line
– t*n*	change interval between repeat replies to sender. (**1 week** default)
n	append **s** for seconds, **m** for minutes, **h** for hours, **d** for days, **w** for weeks

VAL — Validate SCCS Files
% **val** [*options*] *files*
    command lines read from **stdin** if *files* is –
Options:

– m*text*	*text* is compared with value of **%M%** keyword
– r*sid*	specify SCCS ID of version
– s	suppress **stdout**
– y*text*	*text* is compared with value of **%Y%** keyword

VALDATE — Validate Date
% **/usr/sadm/bin/valdate** [**-f** *fmt*] [*input*]
(see also **ckdate**)
Options:

– f *fmt*	input format:
	%b abbreviated month name
	%B full month name
	%d day of month (01-31)
	%D date as %m/%d/%y (default)
	%e day of month (1-31)
	%h same as **%b%**
	%m month number (01-12)
	%y year within century
	%Y year (4 digits)
input	input to be verified against format criteria

VALGID — Validate Group ID
% **/usr/sadm/bin/valgid** [*input*]
(see also **ckgid**)

input	input to be verified against **/etc/group**

VALINT — Validate Integer
% **/usr/sadm/bin/valint** [**-b** *base*] [*input*]
(see also **ckint**)
Options:
    −b *base*   numeric base (2-36, **10** default)

input   input to be verified against base criteria

VALPATH — Validate Pathname
% **/usr/sadm/bin/valpath** [*options*] [*input*]
(see also **ckpath**)
Options:
−a	pathname must be absolute
−b	pathname must be block special file
−c	pathname must be character special file
−f	pathname must be regular file
−l	pathname must be relative
−n	pathname must not exist
−o	pathname must exist
−r	pathname must be readable
−t	pathname must be touchable
−w	pathname must be writable
−x	pathname must be executable
−y	pathname must be directory
−z	pathname must be non-zero size file

input   input to be verified against validation options

VALRANGE — Validate Integer Range
% **/usr/sadm/bin/valrange** [*options*] [*input*]
(see also **ckrange**)
Options:
−b *base*	numeric base (**2-36**, **10** default)
−l *low*	lower limit of range
−u *high*	upper limit of range

input   input to be verified against base and upper and lower limits

VALSTR — Validate String
% **/usr/sadm/bin/valstr** [*options*] [*input*]
(see also **ckstr**)
Options:
−l *len*	maximum length of input
−r *regexp*	match regular expression with input (multiple permitted; input only need match one)

input   input to be verified against format length and/or regular expression criteria

VALTIME — Validate Time
% **/usr/sadm/bin/valtime** [**-f** *fmt*] [*input*]
(see also **cktime**)
Options:
−f *fmt*	input format:
	%H hour (00-23)

(continued)

VALTIME, continued

%I	hour (00-12)
%M	minute (00-59)
%p	AM or PM
%r	time as **%I:%M:%S %p**
%R	time as **%H:%M** (default)
%S	seconds (00-59)
%T	time as **%H:%M:%S**

input   input to be verified against format criteria

VALUID — Validate User ID
% **/usr/sadm/bin/valuid** [*input*]
(see also **ckuid**)

input   input to be verified against **/etc/passwd**

VALYORN — Validate Yes/No
% **/usr/sadm/bin/valyorn** [*options*]
(see also **ckyorn**)

input   input to be verified as **y, yes, n, no,** in
                   any combination of uppercase and
                   lowercase letters)

VEDIT — VI For Beginners (see **VI**)

VGRIND — Format Program Listings using **troff**
% **vgrind** [*options*] *files*
Options:

−2	two-column output, 8pt type, landscape mode
−d *dfile*	specify definition file (**/usr/lib/vgrindefs** default)
−f	force filter mode - **stdout** suitable for **troff** input
−h *header*	specify page header text
−l*lang*	specify language

c	C language (default)
c++	C++ language
csh	C shell language
f	Fortran language
i	ISP language
I	Icon language
LDL	LDL language
m	Model language
ml	emacs MLisp language
p	Pascal language
r	RATFOR language
sh	Bourne shell language

−n	don't make keywords boldface
−o*list*	print only listed pages
−P*ptr*	send output to printer *ptr*
−s*n*	type size set to *n* points
−t	set **troff −t** option
−T*name*	format for device *name*
−w*n*	set tabs 4 columns (**8** default)
−W	wide (Versatec) output format

(continued)

VGRIND, continued

−x	output index in pretty format
list	comma-separated, *n−m* means range,
	−n means beginning to page *n*,
	n− means from page *n* to end

VI — Screen Editor
% **/usr/bin/vi** [*options*] [*files*]
% **/usr/xpg4/bin/vi** [*options*] [*files*]
Options:

+ *cmd*	execute *cmd* in editor
−c *cmd*	execute *cmd* in editor
−C	work with encrypted file (simulate C cmd)
−l	set up for editing LISP programs
−L	list filenames of files saved in crash
−r *file*	retrieve last saved version of *file*
	after system or editor crash (list of all
	saved files default)
−R	read-only mode (same as **view**)
−l − **s**	suppress all interactive user feedback
	(useful with editor scripts)
−t *tag*	edit file containing *tag* and position editor
	at its definition
−vn	display editing state (default)
−Vn	verbose
−wn	set default window size to *n*
−x	create or edit encrypted file
pos	any editor command not containing a
	space

VIEW — Read-only **vi** (see **VI**)

VOLCHECK — Checks for Media in Drive
% **volcheck** [**options**] [*path*]
Options:

−is	frequency of device checking *s* seconds
−ts	check devices for next *s* seconds
−v	verbose

φ **VSIG** — Synchronize Co-process with Controlling
Application
% **vsig**
send **SIGUSR2** signal to controlling FMLI process

W — Who Is Logged In and What Are They Doing
% **w** [*options*] [*user*]
Options:

−h	suppress heading
−l	long form output (default)
−s	short form output
−u	produce heading with time and uptime
−w	produce long form of output (default)
user	restrict output to *user*

ξ **WAIT** — Wait for Background Process to Complete
% **wait** [*pid*]

pid process ID

κ **WAIT** — Wait for Background Processes to Complete
% **wait** [*pids*]

pids   process IDs

σ **WAIT** — Wait for Background Process to Complete
% **wait** [*pid*]
% **wait** [%*jid*]

jid job ID
pid process ID

WALL — Broadcast to All Users
% **/usr/sbin/wall** [*options*] [*file*]
    message read from **stdin** if no *file* specified
Options:
    – a   broadcast to console and pseudo-
                 terminals
    – g *grpnm*   broadcast to specified group by name
                 grpnm only

WC — Count Lines, Words and Characters
% **wc** [*options*] [*files*]
    stdin read if no *files* specified
Options:
    – c   output byte counts
    – C   output character counts
    – l   output line counts
    – m   output character counts
    – w   output word counts

WHAT — Print SCCS Identifying Information
% **what** [*option*] *files*
Option:
    – s   print only first occurrence of pattern

WHATIS — Display Summary About Keyword
% **whatis** *keyword*

WHENCE — Get Shell Environment Values
% **whence** [*options*] [*names*]
Options:
    – p   path search despite alias, function,or
                 reserved word
    – v   verbose

β **WHEREIS** — Locate Binary, Source & Man Page Files
    for Command
% **/usr/ucb/whereis** [*options*] [*files*]
Options:
    – b   search only for binaries

(continued)

WHEREIS, continued

– B *directory*	change or otherwise limit search for binaries
– f	terminate last directory list and signal start of file names; mandatory with options **B**, **M**, and **S**
– m	search only for man page sections
– M *directory*	change or otherwise limit search for man page sections
– s	search only for sources
– S *directory*	change or otherwise limit search for sources
– u	search for unusual directories

WHICH — Display Pathname of Command
% **which** *filenames*

ξ **WHILE** — Conditional Looping Command
% **while** (*conditions*)
actions
end

κσ **WHILE** — Conditional Looping Command
See **Control Commands** in the Solaris SHELL section
Pages 168-172

WHO — Who is on the System
% **/usr/bin/who** [*options*] [*file*] [**am i**]
% **/usr/xpg4/bin/who** [*options*] [*file*] [**am i**]
Options:

– a	turn all options on
– b	list time and date of last reboot
– d	list expired processes not respawned by **init**
– H	print column headings
– l	list lines available for **login**
– m	display only information about current terminal
– n *n*	display *n* users/line
– p	list active processes spawned by **init**
– q	quick; only names and user count
– r	list info on run-level of **init** process
– s	list current users' name, line and time logged in (default)
– t	show last time **date** changed clock
– T	list info on state of terminal
– u	long list of info on logged in users
file	read instead of **/var/adm/utmp** for login information
am i	outputs who you are logged in as

β **WHOAMI** — Display Effective Username
% **whoami**

WHOIS — Internet Name Directory Service
% **whois** [*option*] *name*
Option:
    –h *host*   search on specified host

name can be a user name or handle
.*name*	matches user name only
!*name*	matches handle only
*name	matches group or organization
name...	matches anything beginning with *name*

WRITE — Write to Another User
% **write** *user* [*tty*]

XARGS — Construct Argument List and Execute
% **xargs** [*options*] [*cmd* [*initial_args*]]
Options:
–e [*eof*]	set end of file string (underscore default)
–E *eof*	set end of file string (must be specified)
–i [*replace*]	*cmd* executed with occurrences of *replace* in **stdin** replaced by *initial_args*
–I *replace*	same as -**e** but *replace* has no default and must be specified
–l [*n*]	*cmd* executed for each *n* lines of arguments
–L *n*	same as -**l** but *n* has no default and must be specified
–n *n*	*cmd* executed with up to *n* arguments
–p	prompt user whether each *cmd* invocation is to be executed (**y** confirms execution)
–s *n*	max size of any argument list is *n* characters (470 default)
–t	trace; executed *cmds* output to **stderr**
–x	stop if any argument list greater than size *n* characters

XGETTEXT — Extract **gettext** Strings from C Program
% **xgettext** [*options*] *files*
Options:
–a	extract all strings
–c *ctag*	comment block beginning with *ctag* added to output **.po** file
–d *ofile*	rename default output file to *ofile*.**po** (**messages.po** default)
–h	display help message
–j	join (append/merge) new messages with contents of file
–m *prefix*	prepend *prefix* to *msgstr*
–M *suffix*	append *suffix* to *msgstr*
–n	add comments indicating source of messages
–p *dir*	place output files in *dir* (current directory default)
–s	sort output by message IDs; remove duplicates

(continued)

XGETTEXT, continued
> **– x** *xfile*   *xfile* is **.po** format file
> containing *msgids* to exclude

file file from which to extract message strings

XHOST — X Server Access Control
% **xhost** [*options*]
Options:
> **+**   grant access to all
> **–**   restrict access to those in hosts list
> **–** *hostname*
> remove *hostname* from machines allowed
> to connect to server
> *hostname*   add *hostname* from machines allowed
> to connect to server

XINIT — X Window System Initializer
% **xinit** [[*client*] *options*] [- - [*server*] [*display*] *options*]

XSTR — Extract Strings to Implement Shared Strings
% **xstr** [*file*] [*options*]
Options:
> **– c** *file*   take C source text from *file*
> **– l** *array*   specify named *array* in program
> references to abstracted strings
> **– v**   verbose

file take C source text from *file*

XTERM — Terminal Emulator for X
% **xterm** [*tkopts*] [*options*]
Options:
> **.OK**
> *geom*   preferred size and position of
> Tektronix window
> **– ah** *n*   always highlight text cursor
> **+ ah** *n*   highlight text cursor based on focus
> **– aw**   autowraparound allowed
> **+ aw**   autowraparound not allowed
> **– b** *n*   set inner border width to *n* pixels
> (**3**-**40**; **3** default)
> **– bd** *color* set window border color
> **– bg** *color* set window background color
> **– bw** *n*   set width in *n* pixels of
> border surrounding window
> **– cc** *ccr:v* set classes indicated by given ranges
> **– cn**   newlines not cut in line-mode selections
> **+ cn**   newlines cut in line-mode selections
> **– cr** *color* set cursor color (default same as text)
> **– cu**   work around **curses** bug with **more**
> **– C**   display messages sent to console via
> log driver on this window
> **– display** *display* specify X server to contact
> format is
> *hostname***:***displaynumber*[*.screennumber*]

(continued)

XTERM, continued

– e *prog* [*args*]	run *prog* with *args* arguments in this window; return **0** on completion (user's shell, default) Must be last option on command line
– fb *font*	font for bold text
– fg *color*	set window foreground color
– fn *font*	set window font
– geometry *geometry*	preferred size and position of the VT102 window; see *geometry* below
– iconic	start as icon rather than window
– j	use jump scrolling (default)
+ j	use smooth scrolling
– l	log output
+ l	do not log output
– lf *logfile*	set log file to *logfile* (**xtermlog.**nnnnn default); if *logfile* begins with I, pipe to specified program
– ls	start shell as login shell
+ ls	start shell as subshell
– mb	enable margin bell
+ mb	disable margin bell (default)
– mc *ms*	set maximum time in *ms* milliseconds between multi-click selections
– ms *color*	set mouse pointer color
– n *str*	set **xterm**'s icon name to *str* (**xterm** default)
– name *name*	set application name (cannot contain "." or "*" characters)
– nb *n*	set right margin (for bell) to *n* (**10** default)
– r	simulate reverse video mode
– rv	reverse video simulated by swapping background and foreground colors
– rw	enable reverse wraparound
+ rw	disable reverse wraparound (default)
– s	xterm may scroll asynchronously
– sb	window has scrollbar (default)
+ sb	window does not have scrollbar
– sf	Sun function key escape codes generated
+ sf	standard function key escape codes generated
– si	output to window repositions screen to bottom of scrolling region
+ si	output to window does not cause it to i scroll to the bottom
– sk	reposition to bottom of scroll region at press of key
+ sk	don't reposition to bottom of scroll region at press of key
– sl *n*	number of scrolled off lines to save (**64** default; 256 max)
– S *ccn*	set last two letters in name of pseudoterminal, along with number of inherited file descriptor

(continued)

160

– t	start xterm in Tektronix mode
+ t	start xterm in VT102 mode
– title *title*	set window title to *title*
+ tm *list*	bind *list* of terminal setting keywords to characters that should be bound to those functions (intr,quit,erase, kill,eof,eol,swtch,start,stop,brk,susp, dsusp, rprnt,flush,weras,lnext, along with ^@,^a,^b,...^? allowed)
+ tn *term*	set **TERM** to *term*
– T *title*	set window title to *title*
– ut	don't write to */etc/utmp*
+ ut	write to */etc/utmp*
– vb	enable visual bell
+ vb	use audible, not visual, bell (default)
– w *n*	equivalent to - **bw**
– wf	**xterm** waits before starting subprocesses
+ wf	**xterm** doesn't wait before starting subprocesses
+ xrm *rstr*	specify resource string *rstr*

geometry	*n1***x***n2***s1***n3***s2***n4*
n1	horizontal pixel size
n2	vertical pixel size
s1	- indicating pixel offset from right, + offset from left
n1	horizontal pixel offset
s2	- indicating pixel offset from bottom, + offset from top
n2	vertical pixel offset
tkopts	X toolkit options

YACC — Yet Another Compiler Compiler
% **/usr/ccs/bin/yacc** [*options*] *file*
Options:

– b *fprefix*	use *fprefix* instead of **y** for output files
– d	**#defines** for token names and codes to **y.tab.h**
– l	no **#line** constructs in **y.tab.c**
– p *sprefix*	use *sprefix* instead of **yy** for as prefix for external names
– P *parser*	use *parser* as parser
– Qn	suppress tool ID information (default)
– Qy	put tool ID information in output
– t	include debugging code in **y.tab.c**
– v	parse tables and grammar reports to **y.output**
– V	print version information

YPCAT — Print Values from NIS Database
% **ypcat** [*options*] *mname*
Options:

– d *domain*	specify different domain

(continued)

YPCAT, continued

> **–k**   display keys for maps with null values
>   or key not part of value

mname   map name or nickname

YPMATCH — Print Key(s) from NIS Map
% **ypmatch** [*options*] *key mname*
Options:

> **–d** *domain* specify different domain
> **–k**   print key name followed by ; before value
> **–t**   inhibit map nickname translation
> **–x**   display map nickname table

key   key name of interest
mname   map name or nickname

YPPASSWD — Change NIS Password
% **yppasswd** [*username*]

YPWHICH — Return NIS Server Name
% **ypwhich** [*options*] *hostname*
Options:

> **–d** *domain* specify different domain
> **–m** [*mname*]
>   find master NIS server for map;
>   if no *mname*, produce list of
>   available maps; (*hostname* cannot
>   be specified with **–m** option)
> **–t**   inhibit map nickname translation
> **–V** *n*   version of ypbind in use (3 default)
> **–x**   display map nickname translation table

ZCAT — Display Compressed File
% **zcat** *file*

NAWK/AWK

Abbreviations

ex	arithmetic or string expression
re	regular expression (See Page 173)
str	string
var	awk variable

Program Format
- Program consists of one or more lines like the following:
  - *pattern* { *statements* }

Function definitions have the form:
  - **function** *name*(*var1*,. . .) { *statement* }

- Statements are executed for each pattern that matches current record
- Missing pattern matches all records
- Missing statement prints current record
- Comments start with a # and continue to the end of the line
- Positions and offsets start at 1 (not 0)

Variables
- Variable names start with a letter
- Names can contain letters, digits, _
- Array Reference: *var* [*ex*]
- Built in Variables

ARGC	command line argument count
ARGV	command line arguments (array)
FILENAME	name of current input file
FNR	record number in current input file
FS	input field separator (blank and tab default)
NF	number of fields in current record
NR	number of current record
OFMT	output numeric format (%.6g default)
OFS	output field separator (blank default)
ORS	output record separator (newline default)
RLENGTH	string length from last re match
RS	input record separator (blank means blank line)
RSTART	beginning position of string in last re match
SUBSEP	subscript separator (\034 default)
$0	complete input record
$*i***	field *i* of input record

- Type Conversion
  Automatic between numeric and string
  Force to string: *ex* " "
  Force to numeric: *ex* **+ 0**

Match Expressions

ex ˜ /*re*/	true if *re* matches expression
ex !˜ /*re*/	true if *re* doesn't match expression

Patterns

BEGIN	matches before first record
END	matches after last record
/re /	matches if regular expression matches current record
match	matches if match expression is true
relation	matches if relation is true

- Patterns may be combined with logical operators
- Range of patterns specified as:
  pattern1,pattern2
- ( ) can be used to group patterns

Regular Expressions

c	any character except special chars / ( ) * .	+ ? [ˆ $ matches itself
c	matches special character *c*
nnn	matches char with ASCII value *nnn* octal
.	matches any single character except newline
[*list*]	matches any character in *list* *list* is one or more single chars or ranges specified with –
[ˆ*list*]	matches any char not in *list*
ˆ	anchors pattern match to start of string
$	anchors pattern match to end of string

- Combining Regular Expressions:

(*re1*)(*re2*)	matches concatenated *re*'s
re *	matches 0 or more *re*'s
re +	matches 1 or more *re*'s
re **?**	matches 0 or 1 *re*
*re1*l*re2*	matches *re1* or *re2*
(*re*)	matches *re*

( ) are optional; they ensure precedence

Expressions

- Arithmetic and String Operators:

ex **+** *ex*	add
ex **–** *ex*	subtract
ex ***** *ex*	multiply
ex **/** *ex*	divide
ex **%** *ex*	modulus
+ *ex*	unary plus
– *ex*	unary minus
var **++**	post-increment
var **––**	post-decrement
++ *var*	pre-increment
–– *var*	pre-decrement
(*ex*)	grouping
ex1 ex2	concatenation
ex1 **?** *ex2* **:** *ex3*	conditional

Expressions (continued)

- Assignment Operators:

var = *ex*	assign to *var*
var += *ex*	add to *var*
var −= *ex*	subtract from *var*
var * = *ex*	multiply by *var*
var /= *ex*	divide by *var*
var %= *ex*	*var* modulo *ex*
var ^= *ex*	*var* to the *ex* power

- Relational Operators:

ex1 < *ex2*	less than
ex1 <= *ex2*	less than or equal
ex1 == *ex2*	equal
ex1 != *ex2*	not equal
ex1 >= *ex2*	greater than or equal
ex1 > *ex2*	greater than

- Logical Operators (can use with patterns):

ex1 **&&** *ex2*	and
ex1 ‖ *ex2*	or
!*ex*	not

- Examples of Constants:

5678	integer format
5.43E+21	exponential format
987.654	decimal format
"this is it"	string

Operator Precedence

- Highest to Lowest
- Parenthesis can be used to reorder precedence
- **:?** and ^ are right associative; all others are left

$	(field)
++ −−	
^	
+ − !	(unary)
* / %	
+ =	
string concatenation	
< <= > >= != ==	
in	(array membership)
&&	
‖	
:?	
= += −= *= /= %= ^=	

165

Statements
- Statements end with ; , } or <newline>

- Flow of Control:
break	exit enclosing **while** or **for**
continue	next iteration of **while** or **for**
delete *var*[*ex*]	remove element *ex* from array *var*
do *stmt* **while** *expr*	
exit[*ex*]	exit awk; return *ex*
for ([*ex1*]; [*ex2*]; [*ex3*]) *stmt*	
for (*var* **in** *array*) *stmt*	
	step through array
if (*ex*) *stmt1* [**else** *stmt2*]	
next	skip to next record
return [*ex*]	
while (*ex*) *stmt* repeat *stmt* while *ex* is true	
{ *stmt* . . . }	grouping

- Arithmetic Functions:
atan2(*ex1*,*ex2*)	arctan of *ex1*/*ex2* in radians
cos(*ex*)	cosine of *ex* radians
exp [(*ex*)]	exponential function (base **e**)
int(*ex*)	integer part of *ex*
log(*ex*)	natural log of *ex*
rand()	pseudo-random number on interval (0,1)
sin(*ex*)	sine of *ex* radians
sqrt(*ex*)	square root of *ex*
srand([*ex*])	new seed for rand (default = current time)

- String Functions:
  If *ex* is optional the default is **$0**.
  In **sub** & **gsub**, **&** in *str1* is replaced by substring matched by *re*

gsub(*re*,*str1*[,*str2*])	globally substitute *str1* for *re* in *str2* (returns number of substitutions)
index(*str1*, *str2*)	position of *str2* in *str1* (returns offset if found; 0 otherwise)
length [(*ex*)]	length of string
sub(*re*,*str1*[,*str2*])	substitute *str1* for *re* in *str2*
split (*str*,*a* [,*fs*])	split *str* into array *a* using separator *fs* (**FS** default)
sprintf (*fmt* [,*ex* . . .])	returns expressions formatted by *fmt*
substr (*str*,*pos* [,*len*])	substring (*len* defaults to remainder of *str*)

Statements (continued)
- Input/Output Functions:
  - **close**(*ex*) close file or pipe
  - **getline** set **$0** to next input record;
  - set **NF**, **NR**, **FNR**
  - **getline** <*file* set **$0** to next record of file; set **NF**
  - **getline** *var* set *var* to next input record;
  - set **NR**, **FNR**
  - **getline** *var* <*file*
    - set *var* to next record of *file* (returns 0 on EOF, -1 on error, 1 otherwise)
  - **print** ([*ex1* [,*ex2* . . .]])
    - print expressions (**$0** if no expressions)
  - **printf** (*fmt*[,*ex1* . . .])
    - print using C-like format
- Printing functions can be redirected with > and >>
- ( ) are optional on **print** and **printf**
- one statement may be piped using | "*cmd* "

- Print Format Conversions:
  - **%c** character
  - **%d** decimal
  - **%e** exponential notation
  - **%f** floating point
  - **%g** shorter of **%e** or **%f**
  - **%o** unsigned octal
  - **%s** string
  - **%x** unsigned hexadecimal
  - **%%** print %
  - Modifiers:
    - − left justify expression
    - *width* pad field to *width* chars
    - (leading 0 means pad with 0s)
    - *.prec* max string width or number of decimal digits

Solaris SHELL /usr/bin/sh (like Bourne)

Definitions
• *n* – an integer • *name* – the name of a shell variable • *oct* – an octal number • *pat* – explained in conjunction with the **case** command. • *word* – a generic argument; a word. Quoting may be necessary if it contains special characters.

Elaborations
Each command consists of a series of *words*.

Words are terminated by any of the following characters: **; & ( ) I ˆ < > newline space tab**

One or more spaces and/or tab characters are collectively referred to as *whitespace*. *Words* may be separated by any amount of *whitespace*.

A *list* – consists of one or more *pipelines*. These can be separated by ;, **&**, **&&**, II and optionally be terminated by ; or **&**.

A *pipeline* consists of a command or multiple commands connected by a pipe (I), **this connection indicating that the standard output (stdout) from commands to the left of a given pipe is fed into the standard input (stdin) of commands to the right of said pipe.**

Control Commands

case *word* **in** [*pat1*[I*pat2*]...)*list*;;]...**esac**
> execute *list* associated with *pat* that matches *word*
> *pat* is a word that may contain the wildcard characters *****, **?** and [ ]
> I is used to indicate an **or** condition

for *name* [**in** *words*] **do** *list* **done**
> sequentially assign each *word* to *name* and execute *list*
> if **in** *words* is missing use positional parameters

funct **( )** { *list* ; }
> define function *funct*, body is *list*

if *list1* **then** *list2* [**elif** *list3* **then** *list4*]...[**else** *list5*] **fi**
> if executing *list1* returns successful exit status, execute *list2* else ...

(*list*)
> execute *list* in a sub-shell

{*list* ;}
> list is just executed in current shell

while *list1* **do** *list2* **done**
> execute *list1*; if last command in *list1* had a successful exit status, execute *list2* followed by *list1*; repeat until last command in *list1* returns an unsuccessful exit status

until *list1* **do** *list2* **done**
> like **while** but negate termination test

Parameters

$n	use positional parameter *n*
$*	all positional parameters
$@	all positional parameters
"$*"	equivalent to "$1 $2 ..."
"$@"	equivalent to "$1" "$2" ...
$#	number of positional parameters
$-	options to shell or by **set**
$?	value returned by last command
$$	process number of current shell
$!	process number of last background cmd
$CDPATH	search path for **cd** command
$HOME	home directory for **cd** command
$IFS	field separators (**space**, **tab**, **newline**)
$LANG	name of current locale
$LC_ALL	locale specs that override all others
$LC_CTYPE	
	locale specific handling of characters
$LC_MESSAGES	
	locale specific handling of messages
$MAIL	name of a mail file, if any
$MAILCHECK	
	check for mail every *n* seconds
	(**600** default)
$MAILPATH	
	filenames to check for new mail
	(: separator; *filename* may be followed
	by %*message*)
$PATH	command search path
$PS1	primary prompt string (**$**)
$PS2	secondary prompt string (**>**)
$SHACCT	accounting file for user shell procedures
$SHELL	name of default shell
name = *word*	
	set *name* to specified word
$*name*	reference to shell variable *name*
${*name***}**	use braces to delimit shell variable name
${*name***:-** *word***}**	
	use parameter *name* if set and non-null,
	else use *word*
${*name***:=** *word***}**	
	as above but set *name* to *word* also
${*name***:?** *word***}**	
	use *name* if set and non-null, otherwise
	print *word* and exit
${*name***:+** *word***}**	
	use *word* if *name* set and non-null,
	otherwise use nothing

Note: using *name* **:** instead of *name* checks if *name*
is set and non-NULL; using *name* checks
only if *name* is set

Input/Output

All of these operators may be preceded by an optional file descriptor.

Defaults are shown in parentheses.

<*file*	use *file* as **stdin** (fd0)
>*file*	use *file* as **stdout** (fd1)
>>*file*	like > but append to *file* if it exists
<&*n*	duplicate input file descriptor from *n* (**stdin**)
>&*n*	duplicate output file desc. from *n* (**stdout**)
<&–	close **stdin**
>&–	close **stdout**
<<*word*	use following lines as **stdin** until line with *word* encountered

If any of *word* is quoted, no additional processing is done on input by shell. Otherwise:

- parameter & command substitution occurs
- escaped newlines are ignored
- a \ must be used to quote \, **$**, '

<<– *word*	as above with leading tabs ignored

Special Characters

|	pipe – connects two commands
;	command separator
&	run process in background; default **stdin** from **/dev/null**
&&	only run following command if previous command completed successfully
||	only run following command if previous command failed
'	enclose string to be taken literally
"	enclose string to have parameter and command substitution only
`	in-line command execution
\	ignore special meaning of following character
?	match single character in filename
*	match 0 or more characters in filename
[*chars*]	match any of *chars* (pair separated by a – matches a range)
[!*chars*]	match any except *chars*

Built-in Commands – simple commands executed by sh

#	start of comment; terminated by newline
. *file*	read and execute commands from *file*
:	null command; returns 0 exit status
[*cond*]	see **test**
break [*n*]	exit from enclosing **for** or **while** loop
cd [*file*]	change current directory to *file*
continue [*n*]	
	do next iteration of enclosing **for** or **while**
echo [*words*]	
	echo *words*
eval [*words*]	
	evaluate *words* and execute result
exec [*words*]	
	execute *words* in place of shell
exit [*n*]	exit with return value *n*
export [*names*]	
	export *names* to environment of commands
getopts	parse parameters and options
hash [– **r**] [*files*]	
	remember locations of *files*;
	if no *files* show hash info
	– **r** forget all remembered locations
login [*words*]	
	same as **exec login** *words*
newgrp [*words*]	
	same as **exec newgrp** *words*
pwd	print working directory name
read *names*	
	read **stdin** and assign to *names*
readonly [*names*]	
	mark *names* read-only; print list if no *names*
return [*n*]	exit with return value *n*; with no *n* return status of last command
set [– *options*] [*words*]	
	set flags (**aefhkntuvx**– are valid) (see **sh** command);
	words set positional parameters
set [+*options*] [*words*]	
	unset flags (see **sh** in Commands section)
shift [*n*]	rename positional parameters; $n+1=$n ... (*n* defaults to 1)
stop *pids*	halt processes with specified *pids*
test	evaluate conditional expressions (see **test** in Commands section)
times	print accumulated process times
trap [*word*][*sigs*]	
	execute *word* if signal in *sigs* received
	no *word* or *sigs* – print traps
	no *word* – reset *sigs* to entry defaults
	word is null string – ignore *sigs*
	sigs is **0** – execute *word* on exit from shell
type	*files* show how shell would interpret each *file*

ulimit [*type*] [*options*] [*limit*]

           type (default is both):
                  – **H** hard limit
                  – **S** soft limit
           options:
                  – **a** all (display only)
                  – **c** core file size (512-byte blocks)
                  – **d** "k" of data segment
                  – **f** file size (512-byte blocks)
                  – **n** maximum field descriptors +1
                  – **s** "k" of stack segment
                  – **t** cpu seconds
                  – **v** "k" of virtual memory

umask [*oct*]

           set file creation permissions mask
           to complement octal *oct*
           (see **chmod** for details of *oct*)

unset [*names*]

           unset variables or functions *names*

wait [*n*]   wait for process *n* ; if no *n*, wait for all
           children

Job Control

If invoked as **jsh** the following additional commands
are available.

jobid	the job identifier for a job:
%	current job
+	current job
–	previous job
?*str*	job uniquely identified by *str*
n	job number *n*
pref	job whose command line begins with *pref*

jobid defaults to the current job

bg[**%***jobids*]

           resume execution in background

fg[**%***jobids*] resume execution in foreground
           or moves background job to foreground

jobs [*option*] [**%***jobids*]

           report status of stopped/background jobs
                – **l**   report PGID and current dir of jobs
                – **p**   report only PGID of jobs

jobs – **x** *command* [*args*]

           replace *jobid* in *command* or *args* with
           PGID and execute *command* passing *args*

kill [– *signal*] **%***jobid*

           built-in version of kill for job control

kill – **l** list signal numbers and names

stop **%***jobids*

           stop specified background jobs

suspend   suspend execution of current shell

wait [**%***jobids*]

           wait that uses *jobid*
           if **%***jobid* missing it behaves like
           regular wait

REGULAR EXPRESSIONS

Regular expressions are used in many UNIX utilities: **vi**, **ed**, **sed**, **grep**, **egrep**, and **awk**.

Regular expression characters overlap with shell metacharacters. You can use single quotes to "insulate" them from shell interpretation.

Summary of Regular Expressions In Decreasing Precedence	
c	if non-special char, matches itself
\\c	turn off special meaning of c
^	beginning of line
$	end of line
.	any single character
[...]	any one character in ... or range
[^...]	any one character not in ... or range
\\n	what the n'th \\(...\\) matched (grep only)
r*	zero or more occurrences of r
r+	one or more occurrences of r (egrep only)
r?	zero or one occurrences of r (egrep only)
$r1$l$r2$	$r1$ or $r2$ (egrep only)
\\(r\\)	tagged regular expression only (grep only)
(r)	regular expression (egrep only)